# A LIFE IN SERMONS

## By

# Rev Ian Atkinson

*Collated by Lesley Wilson.*

*Supported by Rivendell Care Home, Birnam.*

*Cover design by Jan Harrison.*

*For Julie S McEwen without whom this book would never have been written. Thank you for you inspiration and encouragement.*

# Contents.

**Part 1 – Autobiography**

**Part 2 – Sermons**

# Resurrection

## By

## Ian Atkinson.

I will die

My life will end

And I shall be no more

No, no I cry – this cannot be

I am, I dream, I yet will be

Can every glimpse of beauty seen

Can every flash of truth I glean

Can every touch of love I chart

Can every longing of my heart

In the end lead nowhere,

Mean nothing, never be complete?

These longings of the spirit

This journey of the soul

Must surely find fulfilment

Must end in what is whole.

This body – it can moulder

Its atoms all decay,

But the spirit then has freedom

To live another way.

Time is but earth's measure

Of change from birth to death.

Eternity is the atmosphere

In which the soul draws breath.

This body makes me earth bound

It makes me grave bound too

But the spirit cannot so be prisoned

And must the grave pass through.

This is the Saviour's promise

Who himself rose from the dead

That raised from its earthly resting place

My self shall rise above

To those passed on before me

To the Saviour who will meet me

In the eternal light and glory

Of the heavenly Father's love.

# Autobiography.

I was born in the village of Bowdon near Altrincham in Cheshire in 1933 and followed a journey through kindergarten, local primary school, prep school at Horris Hill near Newbury, Winchester College, National Service and University. At Oxford I went to Brasenose College, I haven't the slightest idea why I chose that College, I think the House Master at Winchester may have suggested it. My father had been at New College so it wasn't him. Originally my parents wanted me to follow my father and my grandfather's footsteps into law but at a young age I knew that I didn't want to do a job that involved standing up in front of people. I was shy as a child, like my father, the family joke was that my mother had to ask him to marry her.

There was never any pressure placed on me to study law and on the day that I walked into St Benedict's in Manchester for the first time and listened to the priest I felt so at home that I knew there and then what I would do with my life. Father was rather pleased about my choice as he was a deeply religious man himself, we didn't talk about it, we didn't talk an awful lot but we always enjoyed each other's company; playing golf, working in the garden and doing the washing up together. Every year around

Easter time we would go on holiday to Wales or the Lake District and enjoyed many family walks together.

Family holiday at the Lake District.

Home was a quiet, safe, and happy place. Mother was a calm, quiet woman, very slim and not very tall. She had been born in India as her father was based there and at a very young age was sent to live with a Great Aunt in Dundee. She had a brother and two sisters, one sister had died at the age of 21, Uncle Oswald was father's best friend at university, that's how he met my mother. Although she was quiet, she was always the boss, she was always there and never got in a temper. She was the bedrock of our family.

Father was called up when the second world war was declared, Patricia and I were around six and Eileen a couple of years older, he didn't return home again for six years. He spent all of the war years in India, he was never in action and so I wasn't worried about him in that sense, but when the war ended instead of being demobbed he was sent to Germany to work on the war crimes trials. Mother wrote to him frequently, she was a great letter writer and would spend many hours quietly writing, he wrote regularly and we wrote weekly letters back to him. We accepted him being away he had been away for such a long time that that was our norm. During the war years, at boarding school, the master kept us up to date on what was happening and when we returned home we could hear the bombing in Manchester.

Patricia and I are twins and we spent all our time together, we'd play tennis and spend time outdoors, gardening. In the little house in Cheshire we had a small greenhouse which we divided into three but Eileen wasn't really keen on gardening, she loved the piano, and so Patricia and I divided it in half and spent hours and hours working in the greenhouse. Once we moved to Scotland we had nine acres to enjoy.

Ian and Patricia.

As twins Patricia and I supported each other, although I played prop more than she did, I'm the older twin but she's definitely the boss. Her attitude was always, I know what I want and nobody is going to stop me. I'm lucky that I'm self-sufficient, somewhat reserved, but I've always been content with who I am and keeping my own counsel, my father was like that too. Patricia wasn't like that, that's why she made such a good nurse, she'd talk to anyone, if we got into a taxi she'd talk straight away whereas I didn't talk at all if I were alone in a taxi. We were very reliant on each other although she was more reliant on me and I gave her support throughout her life but I always had a need to go to her and spend time with her, be with her, it was part of the two of us being one. At kindergarten we sat next to each other and I did quite a lot of arithmetic for her, if she got stuck she'd nudge me and I'd tell her the answer. The troublesome ones were up the back of the class so the teacher never noticed us in the front. The first time we were separated was at age eight when we were sent to boarding school, she was sent to a girls' school which luckily was the same school as Eileen. I was a good letter writer and I'd regularly send letters to home, to Patricia, and to Eileen.

Returning home for the holidays was always a joy. One Christmas when Patricia and I were around twelve, and hadn't seen our father for six years, mother told us that he was coming home for Christmas but not exactly when. We were both upstairs when she shouted, 'Ian, Patricia it's Daddy!' We ran down the stairs and standing at the door was a tall man in a grey coat and mother was in his arms. He wasn't strange after a second or so and I rushed over to greet him but Patricia screamed, 'That's not my Daddy!'. However, as soon as he picked her up and gave her a kiss she was alright, I don't know what he said to her, we all went to sit around the fire. It is my happiest Christmas memory.

In 1958 my family moved to Perthshire in Scotland, to Dalbeathie House nestled between Dunkeld and Caputh. Father was a country lover and Mother a Scot and the chance of

Dalbeathie at a cheap price was too much to turn down. The first time I saw it I knew that I was home; the grounds were lovely and I was moved by the serenity of it all. It was to be my home until 1993.

Dalbeathie House.

We were well-off as a family and were fortunate to be in a position where our parents paid our way through university. Prior to university I had spent two years with the Intelligence Corps as part of my National Service and was stationed at a Signals Camp in Graz in Austria. All of my life I was either away at school, university or the army and then home and so I didn't live expensively. Once I was ordained I paid for myself and lived in the Parish where I worked. We were all three driven to some form of ministry. Patricia spent her life working as a nurse. Eileen was a very self-possessed person and lived very happily in Edinburgh, she was clever, a fine pianist and very well read. She worked in Government and with the Bishop of Edinburgh. She was happy with her life and was always awfully pleased that when I visited Patricia and I would spend the night with her and we'd all go to a lovely little café at the end of the road. The last couple of years of her life she had cancer and Patricia looked after her, she died whilst in bed reading a book.

Eileen, Patricia and Ian.

As a senior judge, father had witnessed a great deal of violence and cruelty. He was as a judge at the war crimes trials of the Nazis following the second world war and sat on the bench at the trials of both the Moors murderers and the Kray twins. He had been asked because they didn't think that there would be any histrionics, he was a very calm quiet man. He never spoke about it although mother knew it all because she had stayed with him in Chester for weeks on end during the trial of the Moors murderers when they weren't allowed out of their door because of the press. It left a scar with him, witnessing that kind of violence and cruelty inevitably leaves a scar.

Father died in 1980.

Mum and Dad at Dalbeathie.

I was at boarding school from age eight, then Winchester, the Army, Oxford, and Mirfield and was away from home a large part of my life and as a result I was always very much my own person. I was very quiet; I wouldn't say I was lonely I was in my own bubble I suppose. All my life I've been a bit of a loner I didn't get involved in things like societies or groups, at school I had one friend who also went to the same University as me; he was doing history. At University I had another close friend, Bruce, who was a New Zealander and also a vicar. I went to New Zealand twice for three weeks each time, once with Patricia and once with Eileen. We toured around in a little mini-bus and travelled across the North and South Island, when we visited Auckland I popped in to see Bruce and his wife, he was a Bishop by then.

I'm still in touch with my other friend from school and speak to him on the phone, he's a year younger than me and still goes out and plays golf which I'm very envious of.

Following three years at Oxford, where I studied Theology, I began my training at Mirfield Seminary in Yorkshire but I often wondered whilst I was at Mirfield if I was really cut out to be a Priest. When I expressed this I was asked by one of the Priests, 'do you love God? Do you love your neighbour?'.  I knew the answer was yes to the first and then there was a pause and I said, 'well, I try'. His answer was, 'alright then, God looks after that', and we went on from there. Following Mirfield I had two curacies the first at Welling in Kent and the second at Camberwell. All in all training took eight years until my ordination at Southwark Cathedral. By then I was 25 and worked as a Deacon for a year, which is very much an assistant role, I was then Priested which meant that I could take up any role: Chaplain at a University or school or hospital or as Vicar in a Parish. It was at that point that I got my first and only parish at Tooting Beck.

In 1968 I went to work in South Africa. A friend who was also a priest had been planning to travel to a job in Cape Town University and had said I ought to go to South Africa too. In our first year at Mirfield we had to write five thousand words about something important to us, I chose to write about South Africa and apartheid as it was something that the Monks at Mirfield had spoken about. In the end South Africa refused to allow my friend into the country and I was left with his words in my head, 'It's you who ought to go to South Africa'.

When I came off the boat and was coming through customs, I had a sgian dubh in my luggage to finish off my dress kilt. I was told that I couldn't carry lethal weapons into the country but I explained about the kilt and was finally allowed to keep it however, my copy of Black Beauty was banned.

I thought that I knew a lot about apartheid because of the research for the article that I wrote and I had heard a lot about it from the monks at Mirfield who had worked in the prisons in South Africa. I thought I was prepared but writing about something is different from the lived experience. Hell was made by apartheid.

When I arrived I headed to Pretoria, it's a lovely city and where the capital buildings are. I was on the staff of the Cathedral; running youth groups, visiting parishioners and visiting a prison in Zonderwater where my role was to speak to prisoners who requested a visit. I wrote letters for a prisoner to his family which got me in trouble as I wasn't allowed to do that because the prison authorities couldn't read it before I sent it off. In the end they banned me from going into the prison which I wasn't too unhappy about as it had been a challenging experience. During my time there I met two young men who had been up fighting in a war in Angola, northwest of South Africa. During their time there they had raped many black women and beaten up the husbands, when they came back to South Africa they did the same until they were finally caught. On speaking to them I asked what they would feel if someone had done that to their sister or mother, their response was that they were, 'only bloody n*****s and it wouldn't happen to their family as they were perfectly decent white women'. They didn't see black Africans as human beings.

The Dean of the Cathedral was a good man and like many white families had servants who were black Africans and who lived in a hut at the back of the garden. At Christmas he would invite them into dinner but they always said they couldn't, they weren't allowed, and ninety percent of the white families would agree with them. One week the Dean said to me, 'you're preaching this Sunday but we've got trouble with the kiss of peace'. We had a mixed Church with quite a few black people in the congregation, that's what the Anglican Church stood for. However, what was happening during the kiss of peace was that when half of the white people turned around and saw a black person they would turn away. So, in my sermon on that Sunday I spoke of it and told them that the kiss of peace would not happen in this Church. Afterwards I got down from the pulpit pretty smart. Quite a lot of the congregation didn't have a problem with it but some were heard to complain, 'I'm not going to kneel at the altar in the same place as *them*.' It was an ongoing problem and when previously someone in the choir had suggested that we should include black people, the choir went on strike. On another occasion there was an Austrian who had been working with a black orchestra and choir and they were coming to put on a performance of Brahms Requiem in the Cathedral, but some people complained that '*they* couldn't play music, *they* don't understand it.' When the orchestra came to set up, I suggested that they come up to my flat at lunch time as black Africans weren't allowed to go to local coffee shops or restaurants. When two members of the congregation arrived and discovered this they were outraged? 'What's happening here, you're having them in your flat what the bloody hell do you think you're doing? Well, that's the last time you'll see us!'.

And that's how the conflict went on, some whites were utterly apartheid some were very Christian and some backed you up. St Albans College was a white school for boys and one of the teachers occasionally brought the boys to the Cathedral, they came to the Harvest Festival where I talked of the bounties of the earth and how sharing was the best way of expressing gratitude to God and about getting together and collecting donations to give to the poor.

'I didn't have to teach anything else for weeks', the teacher later told me, 'After your sermon all I taught for weeks was about the impact of apartheid'. However, the Head Teacher heard about it and stopped the school coming to the Cathedral; the boys were never allowed to come back to church again.

One time I was driving to a Parish visit when I saw a black African man plodding slowly along the road, I stopped and offered him a lift.

'I can't, I can't!' He said. He wasn't permitted to travel in a car with a white man.

'You can' I replied. 'Get In.'

I drove him for about seventy miles but a mile before we got to where we were going he told me to stop and explained that I couldn't be seen driving a black man, he got out and walked the rest of the way. If you wanted to travel on a train, the first six coaches were for white people the seventh for black people. If you were black you could be a cleaner etc but you couldn't be a train driver. When walking in town with my black African friend I suggested going into a café for a coffee, he grabbed my arm 'We can't! I can't!'

It was ghastly and at one point the Government kicked back at the church and any opposition to them and apartheid, you say the wrong things to the wrong people, or rather the right things to the wrong people and you're out. There were other churches like the Anglicans who refused to accept segregation, the Roman Catholics for example. Not the Presbyterians, they were much more South Africa biased. In the end the Government decided to get its own back on the Anglicans and ruled that all members of the clergy who were out of the country wouldn't be allowed back in and their visas were cancelled: they would never be permitted back to South Africa. I was home in the UK on holiday at the time and although I felt a huge wave of relief I was also torn with guilt. I was relieved that I didn't have to deal with it anymore, that I'd escaped, but it had had a huge impact on me and put me under so much emotional and mental pressure.

When I returned home from South Africa I didn't know what I wanted to do next and didn't feel like doing Parish Ministry. I struggled to know what to do with all the violence and cruelty that I had witnessed and questioned my inadequacies, wondering once again if I was fit for the job. The bishop offered me a parish but I knew that Parish work wasn't for me. I don't think I'm a good priest, I'm not good at talking to new people and the job is about getting to know all of your parish. Even now I'm still as shy as I ever was.

Christ's Hospital, Horsham.

Following a year of recovery at home I began working as Assistant Chaplain at Christ's Hospital in Horsham: an independent boarding school that offered mixed fee paying and charitable places to boys aged 11-18 years. I worked there from 1970 until 1985 and taught the boys Latin, Divinity, coached a hockey team, started a golf team and helped run the Combined Cadet Force (school Corps). I worked seven days a week, I was chaplain, teacher, tutor and as well as all the extra-curricular duties was also House Master for a couple of years. But there were so many other problems to deal with: There were serious problems in the House, I had a very painful back condition, and Patricia was calling me at all times of night and day for support as, since

Father's death, she was looking after our mother who had Alzheimer's Disease. Patricia and I were so close and I felt under so much pressure but I couldn't do anything about father's death, mother's illness, and the trouble at school and once again I questioned my own inadequacies. I sought support from my Parish Priest and gave up the role of House Master. After a couple of years, in order to be nearer to Patricia and mother, I got a job back in Scotland at a Prep School in Broxburn, West Lothian. Although I still worked seven days a week on one day a week I could knock off at six and drive home to spend time with Patricia, stay the night and then drive back in the morning in time for Assembly. That's the thing about that kind of teaching it's not 9-5 because it's boarders and you're on duty all night as well.

After mother's death in 1988 the pressure was off Patricia, and me too. In 1991 I had to retire from school's ministry due to my back trouble, I was fifty-eight and returned home to Dalbeathie. Patricia and I had the whole place to ourselves for two years but one day I looked at Patricia and said, 'it's been an absolute joy but it's suddenly becoming a burden.' She had been feeling the same. We finally sold the family home in 1993 and I moved to a pleasant flat at Druids Park in Murthly where I lived for twenty-five years.

Since my ordination I had preached at St Mary's in Birnam whenever I was home and when I retired I continued to preach there as a non-stipendiary priest, and I also looked after the church garden. Walking trips in Sutherland and golfing were my great pastimes. During my ministry, on my days off, I played golf and in the school I took the boys to different clubs. At Christ Hospital the Old Blues formed a golf club and the individual championship was the Atkinson Cup, which I bought and presented the year I left, they still play for it every year.

Tobermory, Mull.

One day I was at home and I remember getting up and walking through to the kitchen where I grabbed the side and thought, 'uh oh something's wrong.' I picked up the phone and called Dianne and David Simpson and cried 'help!'. They came straight away and the signs of stroke were all there, I was rushed to hospital where I stayed for three weeks. In 2014 I could no longer manage the church garden or play golf and had to retire finally from preaching. When they refused to renew my driver's licence I couldn't get to Dunkeld and I could no longer do the little walk to the shop, so in 2019 I decided to move to Rivendell. I had the great good fortune to move into a little flat which means that I have a lot of independence, I like my own company having lived on my own for sixty years.

Once I moved to Rivendell it all went very well, it was pure providence that the little flat was vacant and I have a little bit of garden that I do, although Frankie the handyman does a lot of it for me and in normal times he could drive me somewhere when I needed to go out and on alternate Wednesdays someone would drive me to Edinburgh to see Patricia to give her moral support, and I'd take along a couple of bags of goodies. She had moved to Edinburgh to look after our older sister, Eileen, who died on New Year's Eve 2010. Sadly, when Covid 19 came along I couldn't go to see Patricia anymore and she was beginning to get confused, she'd ring me up all times of day and night and then she got bad pneumonia and other things that added up in the end. She died in hospital in June 2020 but because of this virus I couldn't be with her. I was able to go to her cremation and she is now buried in the family lair at Caputh.

When I came up here as a young man in 1958 I was newly ordained and later during my holidays I covered services at St Mary's, St Andrews and Strathtay. When I retired and returned home permanently, I was finally able to work in a Parish, and that Parish was my home. My greatest joy was building up a home communion round, visiting and being with the sick and weary who were confined to their own homes. In all I think it added up to regular visits around the Parish to about forty different people. Of all the 1500 services I took in this Parish it was these visits to the home and hospital bound which gave me the greatest joy during my fifty-six years of ministry. All those years to grow into the wonderful family of St Mary's, for all this I have so many happy memories and I thank God for his many blessings.

# Sermons.

The following sermons are a few my personal favourites drawn from over 1500 sermons that I gave throughout my career.

# 1. Sunday before Advent.

Somehow the late Autumn season with its gales and storms, its blood red morning skies, and the mist-shrouded days when hills and forests take on distorted shapes and the rivers seem to smoke is utterly appropriate for the Churches' season of advent which starts today.

Advent is a wild season: a time when Scripture Readings and all those hymns that we know so well strike chords deep in our hearts and touch our deepest emotions. It is a season which disturbs our equanimity as does no other.

As we hear the Scripture Readings with their apocalyptic pictures of portents in the heavens, of nations and peoples lost and bewildered in the surge and roar of the sea and men's hearts failing them for fear: As we sing hymns in which He comes with clouds descending, wrapping all the earth with fear as He comes in judgement. When we are forced to look at our sinful and miserable selves in His pure shining light under which all wrong shall stand revealed who is there among us that is not touched by the first Advent emotion: FEAR.

As we review our lives, our words and actions and know all too well that like those on the judge's left in the Gospel for today we are in the words read by King Nebuchadnezzar in the Book of David, 'Weighed in the balance and found wanting.' What have we to say to that dread judge?

What indeed!

Then in the prophetic readings we hear the repeated refrain of Israel's bondage and longing for deliverance for the oppressed and those who walk in darkness. In the hymns we cry out: 'When comes the promised time that war shall be no more? Oppression, lust and crime shall flee thy face before.' 'Where is thy reign of peace and purity and love?' 'When shall all hatred cease, as in thy realms above?' As we express these feelings we are seized by a deep yearning sometimes almost tinged with despair. The deepest longing of the human spirit for peace and justice; for freedom, forgiveness and wholeness are dragged to the surface.

So Advent sets us tingling with the fear of a guilty spirit yes, but also sets us throbbing with the longing for what the world seems unable to give. But that is not all. Supremely Advent fills the human spirit with hope, a wildly joyful hope.

'The Lord has taken pity on his people.' 'Shout in Triumph for you shall see the Lord.' He comes! 'He comes the prisoner to release in Satan's bondage held.' 'He comes the broken heart to bind the bleeding soul to cure and with the abundance of his grace to enrich the humble poor.' Yes, there is an expectation and an almost wild elation which caps our fear and our longings with a promise of HOPE.

His judgement is a Gospel of forgiveness and renewal to all who turn to him in penitence and faith. His peace and his healing can make us whole for the Kingdom of the Lord who comes is in our individual hearts and minds whenever and wherever we greet him as Sovereign Lord of our lives.

But while Advent in Scripture and Hymnody (both words and the very music itself) is a wild season of conflicting emotions, it is also a time for action as today's reading proclaims.

Fear of judgement demands that we change, that we battle against evil in ourselves with renewed prayer and determination.

The longing of our hearts must become a spur to a personal commitment to the cause of loving humanity in the pursuit of justice and reconciliation and in generous caring service to others.

We do this in the belief that in the Lord who comes, who is the word made flesh, we are not only shown the way but are also called and given the power to share in the bringing in of the kingdom to the hearts of mankind, to bring forward that day when justice shall be throned in might and every hurt be healed.

So as our fear is met by the loving forgiveness of God in Christ, as our deepest longings echo the will of God in Christ and our hope is placed firmly in the power of God so Advent emphasises these three great themes and calls us to action. 'Let every heart prepare a throne and every voice a song,' and could we do better than make our own the words of last week's Collect?

Stir up O Lord we beseech thee the <u>wills</u> of thy faithful people, that they, plenteously bringing forth the fruit of good works, may by thee be plenteously rewarded. Through Jesus Christ our Lord.

Amen.

## 2. Christmas.

On Thursday the Rector made clear for us the relationship between religious fact and story.

If we had sung all 22 of the carols on our Bethlehem card sheets we would if we concentrated on the words rather than the tunes and the enjoyment of old favourites have realised that all of our carols are expressions of the Christian story:

They are awash with angels who represent the heavenly significance of the Nativity. They harp on the Shepherds who represent God's love for the poor and humble: the stars come into their own as they give the Nativity a cosmic significance. Wise Men or Astrologers or Kings come to represent the true light of the Gospel to enlighten even the finest human minds. The animals, the stable, the manger all find their place as God humbles himself in Christ; whilst improbable snow abounds to show the harsh world into which the Saviour comes.

At a deeper level – here and there we sing of the peace; of the healing; of the divine love Christ brings into the world. This is all so good, so right, so heart-warming and joyous that we leave the Church all smiles and cheery to each other. 'What a lovely service Rector – now home to lunch.'

But this won't do my friends, really it won't. Yes, we rejoice in the fact that in Christ God is incarnate in this world. The Word is made flesh – the love, self-giving, sacrificial love of God is poured out in Christ who shares our humanity and is become saviour and purveyor of eternal life. It is indeed right and our bounden duty to give God thanks and praise for our redemption and especially so as we celebrate the incarnation.

But if that is the whole of your response as you leave the Church you have missed out on something of vital importance. Our Carols do manage to hint at it here and there – I quote:

1. 'Ye who now will bless the poor shall yourselves find blessing.'
2. Teach o Teach us Holy child, teach us to resemble thee.'
3. And as we sang just now 'O Holy child of Bethlehem, descends to us we pray, cast out our sin and enter in, be born in us today.'

The incarnation goes on day by day as Christ is born in us so that whatever we receive of God's love in faith, in prayer, in our worship, through the love of others may be passed on by each one of us in daily living. And whether we kneel at the crib, look up at the crucifix, hold out our hands to the Bread of life, always,

always we must hear the voice saying 'As the Father has sent me so now I am sending you.'

# 3. Epiphany.

Since there will be no service next Sunday I thought it would be appropriate this morning to anticipate the feast of the Epiphany which falls on Wednesday. In a way it is no more than a different facet of the Christian festival, it is the more ancient of the two and in the orthodox Church it is Christmas.

But in the West we keep a double feast of the Incarnation. On Christmas day we concentrate on the supreme love of God entering our world in human form – The word made flesh and dwelling among us. At Epiphany we celebrate Christ's revelation to us of the Glory of God - showing forth God's saving power and majesty.

So I think it appropriate that both of today's lessons have been taken from St John – the first from his first letter and the second from his Gospel.

Matthew and Luke give us the birth stories and with Mark then follow Christ's life as Man. All the way through their Gospels neither the disciple nor the audiences nor the opposition – despite moments like the Transfiguration -see Christ as Divine, remarkable though he is in his power and his message. Their narrative is written in what one might call a pre-Resurrection milieu -They come to realise his divinity in the post resurrection Church.

John however writes from the opposite point of view. From first to last, he proclaims Christ the word made flesh, The Son of God, the one who shows forth in word and deed the glory of God in which he shares because he and the Father are one – so that 'he who has seen me has seen the Father'.

In addition to this manifestation of the Father in so many of Christ's utterances we receive the same messages from the seven signs. John does not use the word miracle he talks of the signs Jesus wrought which did two things:

1. Showed forth God's glory.
2. Led people to believe in him.

As we read in the Gospels of God's power reaching out to heal and restore broken lives, to give new hope and vision to those who walk in darkness and promising eternal life to those who accept God's love so we, even today, in the reading of the Scripture see something of God's glory and may be led to faith and find his power to renew and redeem at work in ourselves.

But it never ends there. Christ left his Church to be his body in the world and to continue to proclaim God's power and glory and lead men, women and children of every century back to God. What we have found for ourselves in Christ we must show to others.

However powerful words may be - and they are – whether of a preacher, a philosopher, a teacher, a parent, a friend, a poet or the Scriptures and other literature ACTIONS are more powerful still. Our actions are the true signs of what we are and what we believe and they are powerful in their effects upon those around us, for good and also for evil.

I am humbled again as I meet people whose whole lives have been changed through meeting Christ and the loving, saving, healing power of God through meeting a Christian whose life showed them the divine.

I read of Don Borelli in the slums of Naples; of the 16-year-old Sally Trench climbing down a drainpipe to take food and warm drinks to those asleep on the platforms of Waterloo; of Mother Theresa in Calcutta; of Chad Varah and his Samaritans; of Salvation Army officers in their work with human derelicts and many more in this 20th century.

I have met Trevor Huddleston whose great work was in the Sophiatown slums of Johannesburg; Simon Horne whom I taught at Christ's Hospital- a brilliant classicist- whose life's work is now in a school for deprived children in Zimbabwe; Martin and Alexandra now in the Philippines.

I have seen on television those who have thrown up good jobs and security at home to live and work with mentally disabled Romanian children; with homeless war-battered Kurds; with the starving people of Somalia; with drug addicts in Hong Kong.

Communities, congregations, individuals at whose hands miracles of healing occur today and there are so many others in all three categories whom I could have mentioned. Some of them are not Christians although I think they belong to God even although they do not know it.

But all see human need of various kinds and are called to give all that is in them to meet the needs of those who cry out to receive love and care- help and healing- hope and renewal. Such people are acting on what one might call the heroic scale (although they would never see it that way).

Maybe God does not call those of us here so to act, and because of our age perhaps most of us have given the best years of our lives already to serving God in our various callings. But there is life in us yet and be we in the heroic or the humblest mould we share the same call, that as God's glory was shown to mankind in Christ so now it must be shown in us who are members of Christ, and so we celebrate Epiphany with a two-fold prayer.

First that we may see God more clearly in Christ and be brought closer to him through Christ in faith and prayer.

Second that we may surrender more of our lives to God so that he may be able to show himself not just to us but also through us to his world.

Christ's command to his disciples and to us, 'Let your light so shine before men that they may see your good works and glorify your Father who is in Heaven.'

# 4. Lent.

Today is the last Sunday before Lent starts on Ash Wednesday when at 9.30 communion for all who so wish are signed with an ash cross on their foreheads: a reminder of their commitment to Christ in Baptism and to be worn in public all day as a sign that we belong to Christ and are his witnesses in their world.

I feel also that I should explain the significance of the hymns I have chosen. First we sang 'What a friend we have in Jesus' with recurring refrain 'take it to the Lord in prayer.' This reminds us all that prayer and growth in prayer will be our first and most important search during Lent.

Then we sang 'I to the hills' this a theme in all our readings: Psalm 99 ends 'Praise the Lord our God and worship at his holy hill.' Then Vivienne read us from Exodus of Moses spending forty days in the presence of God's glory before bringing God's law to God's people.

From Matthew came the wonder of Transfiguration at which, even if only momentarily the chosen three Peter, James, and John saw the glorified Christ who spoke of his forthcoming passion and resurrection.

When we reach Lent, we shall meet Christ's wilderness forty days temptation in the mountains of Moab from which he returned and set his face towards the Mount of Olives and the Hill of Golgotha where he must complete the work of our salvation.

For those reasons and my own solitary experiences on the mountain tops of Sutherland I have to refute those lovely words of Dorothy Frances Gurney. 'The kiss of the sun for pardon, the song of the birds for mirth, one is nearer God's heart in a garden than anywhere else on earth.' It is in the deepest moments in solitude that we are most likely to hear the still small voice as our God calls us and speaks to us.

Our third hymn 'Turn back o Man forswear thy foolish ways' emphasises the penitence which must be part of any Lenten devotions.

Finally, because the risen Christ overcomes sin and death and brings to us the promise of eternal life we end by singing 'Thine be the glory'.

So: What are we going to do in Lent as we follow the examples of early Christian converts who used it as a final training course before their Baptism on Easter Day – a practice which before long the whole congregation decided to share both with the converts and their Lord during his forty days in the wilderness?

1. Let us try to be present on Ash Wednesday and receive on our foreheads the badge of a follower of Christ, and perhaps on the other Wednesdays in Lent.
2. Let each of us find some extra time for prayer: either with Bible or the Living Light Bible reading notes for every day or/and time just to be alone with God in prayer and intercession for our world, our congregation, our enemies, our friends, and families.
3. As Christ fasted so let us join him in our own path of self-denial, it may be alcohol or smoking, it may be no little chocolates and titbits, it may be a serious curtailment of our TV watching or some other pleasures of which we have grown over fond. Whatever we decide it is good in our hedonistic world to practice self-denial. And for us all there is the positive side of fasting which makes us remember those millions in the world who fast and starve and die because there is no food, there is no clean water and there are no medicines available.

   This remembrance and prayers which it must occasion should stir us to set aside weekly sums of money which may be given up with prayer and thanksgiving at Easter to be sent to those whom our church decides to support.

4. Christ resisted the temptations of the Devil and we should do the same. For us I think it is quite simple. I am sure you all know the seven mortal sins: pride, covetousness, lust, anger, gluttony, envy and sloth and I would add in a barbed and censorious tongue. So, we look carefully at ourselves. Each of us then may decide, and for most of us I don't think it will be difficult, which /what is our besetting sin and throughout Lent we fight against it seeking ways to conquer it. Each failure we bring to God in penitence and for each victory, however small, we thank God day by day.

Finally, This Lent gives us the opportunity for growth in our faith and God-willing growth in our congregation. None of us should miss this opportunity which this Lent will give us.

May this season of Lent bring us closer to Christ as we seek to follow him with greater faith and love.

Amen

## 5. Jesus' Temptations.

Today's second lesson finds Jesus immediately after his baptism and the divine call; 'Thou art my beloved son in whom I am well pleased.'

Jesus now knew his Messianic mission and immediately, as all gospels tell us, the Spirit drove Jesus into the wilderness, that baked barren highland between Jerusalem, the Jordan, and the Dead Sea.

He fasted forty days and forty nights and faced the temptation of the devil as he tried finally to prepare himself for his mission of Salvation.

We cannot here think of the devil as a horned figure as so often depicted in religious art, we are dealing with an inner struggle, for where the devil attacks is in the inmost thoughts and desires in our own minds. For Christ this was not a once and for all inward battle.

1. At Caesarea Philippi he spoke to Peter, 'Get behind me Satan' the identical words which ended the wilderness temptation, as Peter tried to divert him from his foretelling his death.

2. At the last supper he spoke to the twelve; 'Ye are they which have continued with me in my temptations.'

And then in the Garden of Gethsemane; 'Father, if thou be willing remove this cup from me, nevertheless not my will but thine be done.' Even in the life of him without sin, and who was incapable of sin, this battle was never over until death on the Cross which is why he can help us in our battle with the devil within our minds.

To which of the disciples Jesus bared his soul telling of the temptations in the wilderness we will never know but it is to be a well of compassion and understanding to aid us in our struggles.

So here was the man with all the power of God at his command and it was here that the devil attacked.

The first attack was to turn stones to bread, here was the temptation for the selfish use of Jesus' powers, but more deeply it was the choice by which men could be won to God. In other words, bribery. It was like the promises that politicians make for votes whilst seldom delivering. It is like the parents who say they gave their child everything, except their love, and can't understand why things went wrong. Men's real hunger is not to be satisfied by material things. Hence Jesus' answer from Deuteronomy to the Jews in their 40 years in the wilderness with Moses after the feeding with manna; 'Man doth not live by bread alone but by every word that proceedeth from the mouth of the Lord.'

So next in his mind Jesus stood on the pinnacle of the temple in Jerusalem and the temptation to cast himself down, rise magically unhurt and so amaze men to follow him who had such magical powers, after all the Prophet Malachi had written; 'The Lord whom you seek shall suddenly come to this temple'. And was there not the promise in Psalm 92; 'He shall give his angels charge over thee to keep thee in all thy ways. They shall bear thee up in their hands lest thou dash thy foot against a stone.'

Remarkable feats no more than TV, sports, rock idols can ever change ever fulfil the needs and hopes of men.

Again, Jesus quotes Deuteronomy where we read; 'Ye shall not tempt the Lord your God as ye tempted him in Massah.'

At Massah the children of Israel had got at Moses and God for bringing them into a desert land where there was no water, Finally Moses had struck the rock in Horeb so that fresh water flowed but still it did not answer their questioning, 'Is the Lord among us or not?'

But miracles of the Manna and water did not change the people who were soon back to their own rebellious selves and worse as we shall see from the third temptation.

Finally, Jesus finds himself in his imagination looking over the world he had come to save and the inner voice saying; 'Fall down and worship me and I will give you all the Kingdoms of the world'. In his mind too, the words of Psalm 2; 'Ask of me and I will give the heathen for thy possession.

Jesus' response was immediate and uncompromising; 'You shall worship the Lord your God and him alone shall you serve.' These words, once again from Deuteronomy, take us straight back to the Israelites who when Moses was on the mount to receive the tablets of the commandments made the golden calf; turning to the worship of the pagan God Baal whose worship included prostitution and even human sacrifice. This was the religion of the land they were to enter.

This blasphemy represented the road of compromise with the world in which they lived and is not unlike the current trend of the Christian Church to embrace the secular world's values and practices in the hope of becoming more acceptable to more people!

But the Christian cannot stoop to the level of the world, there can be no compromise. All this lay in Christ's rejection of the wilderness temptations. For men's salvation for expressing God's love to the world and God's will for his people must lead Christ on the path that leads to a cross, a cross which will be and which is his final victory.

## 6. Mothering Sunday.

Tuesday of this week was the feast of the Annunciation which provided the Gospel which I have just read this Mothering Sunday, which is a day of triple thanksgiving, rejoicing and dedication.

First: Hail Mary full of grace, the Lord is with Thee. Blessed art those among women and blessed is the fruit of thy womb Jesus! Many million Catholics both Roman and Anglican/Episcopalian will add to these Lukan/Angelic Words: Holy Mary, Mother of God pray for us sinners now and in the hour of our death. For it was Mary's obedience to God's will spoken by the angel Gabriel – 'Behold the handmaid of the Lord, be it unto me according to thy word': which brought the fulfilment of the prophecy of King Ahaz in our first reading from Isaiah. 'The Lord Himself shall give you a sign. Behold a virgin shall conceive and bear a son and He shall call his name Emanuel.'

So it was that the great work of our salvation through the life and death of Jesus was set in motion. So Mary to whom this church is dedicated is the greatest of Christian Saints and a perfect example to all Motherhood.

Through Jesus' early years Mary fed, washed, comforted and taught the child, was with him at his circumcision on the eighth day of life, an act of dedication akin to that of Baptism, and after 40 days undertook the duty of post birth purification making the offering which allowed the poor to offer a pigeon in place of a lamb for sacrifice.

And so those first years passed until at the age of 12 Jesus went with his parents up to Jerusalem and perhaps for the first time where they returned to find him in the Temple. 'Wist Ye not that I must be about my Father's business.' They and Jesus realised for the first time who he really was. Yet for the next 18 years he returned to his humble home and carpenters trade and during those years Joseph probably died since he is never mentioned again.

But then came John the Baptist and Jesus' Baptism in Jordan and commissioning by God. Still Mary was with him. She it was with the faith to tell the servants at Cana in Galilee to do whatever Jesus told them as he performed his first miracle or Sign as John called it.

Thereafter Mary is mentioned as among the group of women who accompanied Jesus and his disciples in the three-year ministry of healing and preaching. No doubt cooking, mending, helping when needed in those demanding days.

Then finally Jesus' mother was by his cross sharing his pain and suffering, facing the jeering mob and finally being put into the care of John who took her to his own home.

Lastly in the Book of Acts we find Mary and the small group of supportive women in the upper room awaiting the gift of the Holy Spirit.

So for her part in God's work of Salvation Mary is the greatest of the Saints but she is also the pattern for Motherhood.

So secondly, on this Mothering Sunday we all give thanks to God for our mothers, for all they are or have been for us in our lives.

Here I cannot speak for you but only for myself. The centre, the pivot of my childhood in caring, in guiding, in comforting and encouraging was my mother, the only parent I knew from the age of 6 to 13 since my father spent the war years in India and then two further years in the criminal courts in Germany.

Then one day in 1947 a soldier appeared at the front door, mother rushed into his arms and called out to Patricia and me; 'Daddy's back!' We rushed downstairs and there was this tall man in a grey coat and I knew who he was but Patricia cried out, 'That's not my Daddy!'. At which he jumped across the threshold seized her in his arms, lifted her up and kissed her and suddenly all was well.

And so family life settled down and we children grew up and the centre of our lives remained our mother. You will all have your own memories, your own present experience and even for one or two of you the great and joyous duty of loving care and teaching which lies upon you with your own young and growing families. For our memories and responsibilities, we today give thanks to God.

And now Thirdly, Mother Church (well two quotes): Jesus looking on the Holy city of Jerusalem wept over it saying: 'How often would I have gathered Thy children together even as a hen gathereth her chickens under her wings and ye would not.'

Then Paul in our Epistle today speaks of the Church (The body of Christ) saying; 'As we have many members in one body and all members have not the same office, so we being many are one body in Christ and every one members one of another.'

Most completely are we one family as the Body of Christ when we gather together to worship God and meet Jesus in Communion. The Church is a house of prayer where the family gathers and in love and friendship the individual finds strength, finds comfort, finds renewed courage and direction, finds a renewal and deepening of faith from our fellow members in Christ. At other times, and I long for the day when once again St Mary's is open all day, we may come into God's house, our home, alone yet in the company of angels, archangels and all the company of heaven including our own loved ones now with God and find and be with God and so may speak with God and He with us. St Mary's has a real aura of prayer and peace, certainly it has been a home to me now for 55 years and it is 'Mother Church' in that it is the home of the Christian Family of which I am just one member. But a family which is, under God, the source of security, of faith, of service and strength for none of us can stand alone.

So today for Mary Mother of Christ who is our Lord and Saviour

For our own Mothers to whom we owe more than perhaps we can ever measure

For our Church which is both the House of God and also a home to us the children of God

We give thanks today and every day.

Amen.

# 7. Good Friday.

*(Part 1)*

I hope you will not mind me speaking to you from ground level but I feel that like yourselves my proper place is not above but at the foot of the cross.

I have hung Salvador Dali's Galilean crucifixion where I hope you all can see it and find that silent figure leading your thoughts and prayers in the minutes of silent meditation more effectively – I expect than any word which I may have spoken.

Those arms are stretched out wide to embrace the whole world. That cross towers above and overshadows a whole world. Below it is the stillness and calm and the darkness before dawn which belongs only to those who kneel at his feet in penitence and faith to be enfolded in his arms of love.

But why the cross as the key to God's great act of Redemption?

Very simply because it is the final and total proof of the love of God. A love with an infinite capacity to suffer and through its suffering conquer the power of evil and draw human souls to repentance and to return that love with hearts and lives given to God.

All the evil in the world is focused on this figure
– this Christ. All physical pains:

The scourging and nails of vicious punishment
and wracking of torture.

The crown of thorns and beating up by the
soldiers, the ministrations of the bully and the
lover of violence for the pleasure and
amusement it gives. The burden of the cross to
match the weight of the world's and the
burden borne by the poor and the exploited
and the oppressed.

The desperate dying man's thirst, to match the
desperation and deprivation of so many of the
worlds needy.

Even death itself which is to man the final evil.


Mental pains too:

Fear in the garden of Gethsemane at the
prospect of what that night and the following
day held for the Son of Man.

Hatred poured upon him by those who willed
his death and their scorn and mockery when
they had him where they wanted – and this in
religion's name!

The sheer injustice of being found guiltless and
yet handed over to a cruel death sentence.

Betrayal by one of his chosen friends. Desertion by all the rest bar one, and a threefold denial by the leader of the twelve.

Utter impotence as soldiers uncaring rolled their dice for pieces of his clothing and his mother and John stood at his feet powerless to help or assuage his pain even as he was powerless to assuage theirs.

And out of all this is a sense of desolation so great that even God seemed to have deserted him and this is the ultimate weapon of evil against the human soul on the cross.

And so all agony of body, mind and spirit is fastened on Jesus. Yet still the Christ who had prayed 'Father forgive them' did not break but cried in triumph that his work was finished. His Father's will, love's sacrifice was complete and all is commended into the Father's hands.

The cross is in our altars, the cross is on our spires and men pass it by – it was all so long ago. Yet not so! That Good Friday is a reality now – for every day since then until today – for every day from tomorrow until the end of time. Our sin still crucifies Christ in the evil and hurt and rejection which we heap upon our fellow men.


Has killing and torture ended after Pilates judgement?

Has violence and cruelty ended after those Roman soldiers?

Has the burden laid upon the poor as politician, dictator, big business and the con man exploit and rob and crush them ended yet?

Does the cry of the sick, the starving, the homeless yet find relief?

Do people live in less fear today? – Is there yet freedom from racial and religious hatred with their terrible consequences?

Do less people destroy themselves with drugs and ultimately in suicide in their desolation and misery?

No! No! and No!


So sin and evil strike still at all in our world and in striking every individual Christ is struck again – God's love is rejected again – The cross still stands over us in judgement and mute appeal for humanity to turn, to repent, to find God's forgiveness and newness of life.

In this first period of silence (as you sit or kneel in the quiet) I would ask you to use it as a time of intercession, look through the suffering eyes and loving heart of Jesus at the world in which you live – near and far – let him show you when he suffers most in particular evils and pains  inflicted on God's people by sin

– and pray with his compassion for the world's redemption.

Lord Jesus Christ, Son of the living God have mercy upon us (3x)

---------------------------Silence---------------
----------

O Lord forgive the cruelties of men in every age, their insensibility to other's pain. The deliberate act which causes pain to satisfy and to express the evil, that rebels from love's surrender and other's needs in order to exalt itself!

O Lord forgive the carelessness that passes by, the blunted consciences that will not see or fear to see the wrongs we do to others.

O Saviour of the world – who by Thy Cross and precious Death hast redeemed the world...

Save us and help us as we humbly beseech thee O Lord.

Lord Jesus Christ, Son of the living God

Have mercy upon us.

Lord Jesus Christ, Son of the living God

Have mercy upon us.

Lord Jesus Christ, Son of the living God

Have mercy upon us.


------------------------Silence--------------------
---------------

O Saviour of the world

Who by the Cross and precious death

Hast redeemed the world

Save us and help us

We humbly beseech thee O Lord

Let us join in the words of the Prayer Book
Confession – saying it together –

Confession

Absolution

Comfortable words

Hymn 20 vv 2-3

*(Part 2)*

We see on the Cross the love of God in Christ
and the price love pays and must pay in

suffering. But at the same time as we see what our sin does to God we see also his infinite capacity to forgive.

Father forgive them: they know not what they do. It is only when we see and understand the consequences of our sin in the pain and suffering we inflict on others that we know it for the evil that it is and we know too our desperate need for forgiveness.

Judas saw what he had done in betraying Jesus for money – though we will never know the full motive of his actions – and committed suicide in despair at his own vileness.

Peter knew what he had done as he denied Christ and denied his discipleship when challenged, for cowardice had overtaken him. The others with the singular exception of John also fled to disassociate themselves from the condemned yet guiltless Christ. They knew full well what they had done.

Pilate knew too that he had condemned an innocent man because it was expedient. It was the simple way to avoid trouble with the Jews which would be bad for his procuratorship. He even washed his hands in public as an empty gesture to save some self-respect and avoid the blame.

The soldiers praetorian guard who could mock and assault Jesus. And those at the execution detail who rolled dice while a man died in agony beside them – they had learned so to school their emotions that human suffering no longer touched them and the weakness of ordinary people was for them a reason for scorn. They could no longer see the pain and hurt in the eyes of those who suffered at their hands and 'duty' covered any doubts.

The leading Jews...they knew what they did: the man who challenged their authority, who upset their age old pattern of faith and morals and who was getting followers from their flock: That man must be stopped. Where attempts to dissuade him failed they turned to more drastic measures and in the end they had their way. Those were religious people: yet as we read our Gospels the anger, the malice, the envy, the false accusations we find in their hearts and on their tongues is terrible. And when at last they have got their way they are there to gloat in their victory.

One thief curses Christ and seems to blame him for his own – as his companion reminds him – deserved punishment because he cannot and will not accept or face the reality of his own guilt.

And the crowd – so many were filling Jerusalem on their annual visit for Passover – Five days ago many of them were singing and dancing in the procession when Jesus entered

Jerusalem. Now stirred up by the leading Jews and their henchmen they have become part of a mindless mob baying for blood. They have let themselves be swallowed up in the crowd which is so often the death of the individual conscience and the refuge of the weak.

Now many have returned home: the excitement, the madness will soon be forgotten. Just a few who stayed watching to the end may soon be returning home with a sick feeling in their hearts.


Father forgive them

They know not what they do.

But surely they <u>do</u> know what they do and have done! What they do not know is who it is their sin has nailed upon the cross. It is the God of love they have rejected.

Father forgive <u>them</u>.

Much more Father forgive us, forgive me, we <u>do</u> know whom we crucify by our sins. We who art Christians, we who are called to take up our cross to follow Jesus! And yet we still crucify him in the evil we do to others.

As we look at those who crucified Christ, we can see ourselves all too clearly amongst their number. It is only the date and the names and faces of the sinners that have changed.

In the silence gaze upon the crucified and ask him to show you more clearly your sin in lack of faith and love and loyalty to Jesus and in the hurt you cause him by your treatment in thought, word, deed or omission of your fellows made in his image.

Then bring those things which tear most hurtfully at your conscience to his feet in open honesty: offer the best pledge that is in you of amendment and plead for his mercy and forgiveness.

# 8. Easter.

Around us are all the symbolic trappings of Easter as we celebrate Christ's resurrection without which there is no Christianity. As St Paul wrote, 'If Christ be not risen then we have nothing to preach and then you have nothing to believe, all believers who have died are lost and we deserve more pity than anyone else in all the world.'

The white of the vestments and frontals speak to us of great joy; the first flowers of spring speak of nature's renewal of life after winter's deadness; our hymns with their Allelujahs proclaim the Risen Christ who has conquered sin and death and promised us a share in life eternal; Finally, the Paschal Candle speaks to us, with its living flame above the cross and crown of thorns, of the living Christ who dwells in us and we in him.

Today's Epistle is just seven verses which can and should be joyously read again and again, more richly than anywhere else in the New Testament they bring together the fundamental truths and promises of the Gospel. The Epistle is written to the Churches in the Roman provinces of Asia minor and it is written to Christians who fear persecution.

This morning I want to take just three of the themes from these few verses: First the Christian's new life and a living hope which leads us to look forward to the rich inheritance that God keeps for us in Heaven. The writer uses three great pictures to describe this inheritance. The Greek Old Testament uses the word frequently, always referring to the promised land.

Our inheritance Peter writes is far greater for it is imperishable. Many times the promised land was devastated and laid in ruins by alien powers. But Christian inheritance is an inward peace and joy which, however often our faith may falter, no alien power can ultimately ravage or destroy.

Our inheritance cannot be spoiled. Many times the promised land was defiled by the false worship of alien Gods. But the Christian inheritance is a purity and wholeness which, for all the sin of the world and even of our own individual lives, through Divine forgiveness cannot be defiled.

Our inheritance cannot fade away. In the promised land as in any land even the loveliest flower fades and the most glorious blossom dies, even every living creature must sooner or later draw its last earthly breath and return to its dust. Yet our inheritance cannot fade away for it lies beyond the grave where Christ will raise us into a world with himself where there is no change and decay and where our or rather his peace and joy cannot be touched by the evils or the sin or even the ephemeral nature of all the lives of this world.

It is because the Christian possesses God and is possessed by God that he has the inheritance which is indeed imperishable, undefilable and cannot fade away.

And so we can re-write the words of St Paul which I quoted earlier to: We who have faith in the risen Christ deserve more envy than anyone else in all the world.

As I said earlier this Epistle was written to Christians who faced appalling persecution under the Roman Emperors. And so the second theme is the secret of endurance. Peter brings his readers to their actual situation in life.

They are, he writes, to rejoice in their glorious inheritance even though it may be necessary for them to be sad for a while because of the many kinds of trials they suffer: Death in the arena torn apart by lions; death by fire tied to the stake; or death by summary execution; the destruction of their homes, their churches, their scriptures. All these were to be the lot of many of the Asian Christians. But all these sufferings Peter tells his readers have a purpose which is to prove that their faith is genuine. The writer drew the parallel with the testing of gold by fire which could lead to its destruction. So must and will Christian faith be tested so that believers may win praise and glory and honour when Jesus Christ shall appear.

Today and throughout the ages Christians face such suffering both through persecution and in daily living through physical pain, untimely bereavement and other conflicts and misfortunes. Yet the writer in effect reminds them and us of three reasons why we can and shall endure.

1. We can stand anything because of the wonderful inheritance to which we look forward. Even death is not the end.

2. We can stand anything if we remember that all kinds of suffering are tests. In this world trials are not meant to take the strength out of us but rather to put strength into us and enable us to grow.

3. We can stand anything because at the end despite our all too human doubts our all too human sins and our frequent failures to live as God would have us live, we shall if we endure hear those words which mean more than anything else: Well done thou good and faithful servant enter into the joy of thy Lord.

It is for this that we must daily take up the cross, which is the cost of discipleship, the cross which is a sharing of the world's suffering, the cross which is all too often that of our own making and frailty.

Because within and beyond the cross is Easter. The presence of the Risen Christ and the promise of eternal life is with us every day of our lives until the day when we shall finally see God face to face and we shall be complete in Him.

So in faith and joy we raise our heads and sing Allelujah God be praised!

Amen.

# 9. Clean and unclean.

Today's reading from Acts jumps a chapter in which Peter had his vision of the great sheet holding almost every creature that walked, crept, or flew on earth accompanied by a voice saying 'Rise Peter, kill and eat.' Peter's response was a refusal; 'I have never eaten anything common or unclean.' To which response came the voice; 'What God has cleansed do not you reckon common or unclean.' And this vision was delivered three times.

The Jewish food laws were very strict and wide-reaching and written out fully both in Leviticus chapter 11 and again in Deuteronomy chapter 14.

Peter received this threefold vision just after the Roman (Gentile) centurion had despatched two servants to call for Peter to come to him at Caesarea.

It was only on their arrival that Peter realised the import of his vision. Just as the eating of any unclean animal was anathema to any God-fearing Jews: so also was any contact with a Gentile who was regarded as unclean as any proscribed animal.

No devout Jew would ever consider having a Gentile as a guest, let alone entering the house of a Gentile. For me this is a vivid reminder of my days in Vorster's Apartheid riven South Africa and the horrors of some of what went on within the congregation of St Andrew's Cathedral in Pretoria.

One week the Dean of the Cathedral said to me, 'you're preaching this Sunday but we've got trouble with the kiss of peace.' We had a mixed congregation and quite a few black people in our congregation- that's what the Anglican Church stood for. However, what was happening during the kiss of peace was that when half of the white people turned around and saw a black person they would turn away. So I had to preach on that Sunday and in my sermon I spoke of it.

'See how these Christians love one another. When it comes to the kiss of peace, see how these Christians hate one another. The kiss of peace will not happen in this church any longer.' I got down from the pulpit pretty smart. But quite a lot of the congregation didn't have a problem with it. Some of the congregation were heard to complain, 'I'm not going to kneel at the altar in the same place as them.'

Previously someone in the choir had suggested that we should include black people- the choir went on strike. At one point an Austrian had been training a black choir and they were coming to put on a performance of Brahms

Requiem in the Cathedral but some people complained that 'they couldn't play music they don't understand it.' When they came to set up, I suggested at lunch time that they come up to my flat as they weren't allowed to go to any local coffee shops or restaurants. When 2 members of the congregation discovered this they were outraged. 'What's happening here? You're having them in your flat, what the bloody hell do you think you're doing? That's the last time you'll see us!'

Peter realising and accepting the divine revelation granted in his vision, immediately broke all the Jewish laws as he entered the Centurion's home, shared a meal with him and his family and then told them about the crucified and risen Christ who promised forgiveness of sins and eternal life to all who believed in Him.

Even as Peter spoke the Holy Spirit descended upon his audience and Peter ordered that they should be baptised in the name of Jesus.

At this moment a momentous wonder took place, instead of Christianity becoming a Messianic sect within Judaism the Christian faith became open to all mankind, became good news for the world.

Today's reading from Acts tells us of the storm at Jerusalem which greeted Peter's news and action.

So, he had to retell in detail all that had happened and supported this with his quoting of Christ's own words: 'John baptised you with water but you will be baptised with the Holy Spirit.' In face of the words of Christ, of their own experience and what God had done at Caesarea, 'all protest died the death and amid rejoicing it was accepted that God has given life, giving redemption to the Gentiles as well as the Jews.'

So, the Gospel of salvation took its first steps on the road to becoming a world-wide faith. Peter had not so much won an argument as he had presented factual evidence of God's action which could not be gainsaid.

The proof of Christianity does not lie in theological books or discussion: very few people have ever been argued into the Christian faith. Christianity's proof, its power to claim lives for God lies in the fact that it works; it does change men and women, it does make the sinner a new person, it does bring the Spirit of God into human lives and so for you and me our duty, our power to win people for Christ does not lie in theological expertise and words, it lies in the example of lives lived in the power and guidance of the Holy Spirit, in lives lived with the forgiveness and compassion of Christ, in lives lived with the joy of the risen and glorified Christ.

## 10. Rooted.

A few weeks ago we had our storms when broken branches fell and at Dunkeld House, at Rohallion and by the road just short of Stanley shallow rooted trees were felled in swathes.

Before that beyond Murthly school a plantation was felled and a single line of old beeches by the roadside was left alone. Two crashed down in the next high winds because they were shallow rooted and had become isolated.

In the Psalm we spoke of the man who trusts in God as being like a tree planted by streams of water – its roots reaching down to life-giving water and so yielding fruit and prospering with leaves that do not wither.

In the old testament reading Jeremiah uses the identical imagery to describe the man who trusts in God and like a waterside tree stands up to the twin assaults of heat and drought and whose life still bears fruit.

In the New Testament reading from St Luke - in the parable of the sower- the rootless seeds planted on rock withered away through lack of moisture as do Christians who have no real roots and in times of testing fall away.

St Paul too picks up the imagery of roots: describing the Christians at Ephesus as being rooted and grounded in love thus coming to know the love of Christ and being filled with the fulness of God.

And as he writes to the Colossians he urges the Christian Church which has received Christ Jesus the Lord so to live in him...rooted and built up in him...established in the faith which they have been taught to abound in thanksgiving.

So, learning from images of trees, seeds and Christians rooted in love and in Christ perhaps we can gain understanding of our roots as Christians without which we must fall.

First like the lone tree we cannot stand alone. We need to be rooted in our worshipping congregation whence we receive and give support from and to one another.

Like the tree whose roots reach down to water for sustenance so too we must reach down in prayer and sacrament for the power of God to sustain us.

Without community and roots we cannot easily sustain faith or witness in the face of temptation, doubts, hardship, pain or sorrow. So here we know the life-giving power and our need of a living worshipping congregation.

With the corporate strength of the Congregation at worship and in mutual support and caring; and with individual strength from prayer and sacrament we are drawn closer to

God and to one another. But there is more. We are to be rooted- heart, soul, and mind in love – the tap root reaching deep into a knowledge of the power and presence of God in Christ. Without being rooted in love we cannot grow in our union with and knowledge- as St Paul says: - of the breadth and length and depth and height of Christ's love which is to be in us if we would serve the world in his name and his power.

So give a thought to your roots as Christians this Lent. How can you drop them deeper to bring you closer to God and make you more fruitful to his service?

# 11. Retreat.

Most of us can perhaps point to some place which we value for its power to provide us with a retreat or powerhouse where we can reaffirm truths which we know full well yet lose in the hurly burly of daily life, or where we can see things in a truer perspective than we do when under the pressures and demands of our normal routines.

I returned this May as I have done every year since 1970 from the place which along with the altar rail in Communion speaks most clearly to me of just those truths which I most need for peace of mind and for the courage to continue living and loving – or at least endeavouring so to do.

I have returned from four days in Assynt and Sutherland where I walked on and amidst the mountains, idled by waterfall, loch, and river, stood amidst the trees and wild plants, watched and enjoyed the company of birds and other wild creatures – In this Communion with the wild I have received my usual renewal and returned with the thoughts that I would like to share with you this morning.

As I write this, I find myself writing 'I' rather than we or you because it is a personal pilgrimage and renewal. Yet I hope that you will be able to take my 'I's' and treat them as yours.

These marvellous mountains of the North stand unchanged; the same familiar friends today as they were to me thirty years ago. Down their flanks run the same streams and waterfalls to the same lochs, rivers and the sea. There is a permanence and near solitude in this area of Scotland, which I love best, that calms the frenetic soul.

A lifetime for these hills is counted in tens of thousands of years with some of the oldest rocks in the world at one's feet. To these a thousand years is like a minute of your time and mine. How very small, how very impermanent am I and all humanity – 'whose days (as the Psalmist so truly says) are like the grass, which flourishes like a flower of the field, but the wind passes over it and it is gone.'

The divers in the sea and the loch, the Handa puffins, the Inverkirkaig ring plovers, the salmon running the Cassley the Oykel and the Inver, like other creatures and many plants and flowers: these too are there year after year in the same places. Yet these are not like the mountains and the waters. These are a whole succession of generations, for their lifespan is very short. Yet with many fluctuations their race is continued and in a very different way they too will still be there long after I am gone.

Yet all is not the same. New roads and widened roads appear blasted through rock; new houses, chalets and caravans appear whilst old ones are repaired or left to crumble and join the many ruins of the area. Quarries are opened and closed; Cars and lorries in increasing numbers crawl or race along the strips of tarmac ribbon with which man has sought to tame the land.

The hills have watched it all. They watched man come, grow, struggle, depart in the Highland Clearances, clan and world wars; they have watched him labour and enjoy his leisure, they have watched his joys and sorrows, loving and killing, birth and dying. When man goes the weather slowly erodes buildings, nature reclaims his fields and the very rubble of his old crofts until little is left to show his passing. The hills have watched it all.... the whole strange procession which is human history as it passes round their feet and is gone. They have seen it all.

What is it they have seen which speaks to me?

They have seen how far the human race has come along the great road of evolution and progress. If I but think of that progress I know that nothing can happen to me that hasn't happened to countless others. I am just a part of that procession of human history and I share in its progress. When I see life – my life

– against God's time of eternity then the cares and worries of my world with its so-called important events worthy of banner headlines and end of the world type media exposure blazoning events as unique in their horror and urgency or historical decisiveness shrink in significance.

For I know that through- in fact probably because of, our trials and painful circumstances, the human course – my course is upwards. In this certainty the restless soul is calmed and depression is lifted. I am pleased to be a part of this great procession.

A part of this procession. We are all a part and therefore we also have a part to play in this great procession – brief though that part may be. God calls humanity forwards and towards himself.  The Gospel is quite clear that our part as Christians is to love the world as Christ loves us, for that is the path to the Kingdom.

You and I are agents for that Kingdom's coming and, true enough, a pretty good mess we often make of our task. Yet much of our trouble arises from our failure to understand ourselves to be parts of a long, long process. We feel guilt, because of our shortcomings, and failures; we get hurt and angry at lack of response, lack of gratitude or rejection. We are impatient at delay, at opposition at the fact that we can claim no particular measure of success. All this which destroys our peace and our capacity for joy and thankfulness comes from our crazy ideas of our own importance. If I don't succeed, however I quantify success, God's Kingdom fails.

The hills tell me how small I am and that my life is just an incident- in that long procession which with Bronowski or De Chardin we might call 'The Ascent of Man'. Did Christ not call us to be leaven, to be salt, to be a light. Unassuming things yet all noticeable in their effects.

When Lord Burleigh who was a great Christian as well as a historian and philosopher visited South Africa a quarter of a century ago, he visited a country which since the National Party's 1948 victory had been twenty years under the slavery of Apartheid. Informers, police and courts crushed every voice that was raised in the name of human rights or Christian values. Lord Burleigh spoke to a great meeting of Christians and liberals who were bewailing their total failure – in fact total impotence in the face of state repression. Why they asked should God desert them? In words which his audience could not forget he reminded them that the Gospel commanded them to sow, not necessarily to see the crop grow let alone to reap it.

Their reward might be banning or prison or worse – Christ was crucified- the crop/the harvest would come in God's time: not theirs. Their task was to sow.

The recent elections in South Africa are the start of the new crop which we hope will flourish. It is a crop from seed sown over many years in minds and consciences of white South Africans. Few of the original great sowers of the Church and Liberal Party have lived to see their first shoots appear above the ground. Yes, the seed was theirs but the time is God's.

Whenever I revisit Sutherland, I find there a world which is the backdrop to humanity's short history in which human procession has come a long way – much of it arduous – on its upward climb towards its creator.

This fruitful world is also the sustainer of life as generation succeeds generation, handing on its genes, handing on its gifts.

I have a part to play in this unfolding of God's ongoing work of Creation and Redemption and I need not ask what fruits my life will bear. It is enough that I sow what love I can in trust that God will see it – For I am a part of a great whole which moves inexorably towards the Creator. When I am gone the same hills will look down on my successors, a new generation of plants and creatures will sustain and delight them and God's work will go on.

So I come home relaxed and more at peace with myself and my world because I have felt anew the embrace of Eternity – of God's time – and I can repeat with confidence the words of Julian of Norwich ''All shall be well. And all manner of things shall be well.'

So, I say to myself and I say to you, just get on with it disciple of Christ, you haven't very long. But God has all the time there is.

## 12. Prophet Without Honour.

According to St Luke Jesus' ministry began in his hometown of Nazareth in the Hill Country of Galilee. It was much more than a tiny village and if Josephus is to be believed it had a population in the thousands.

If as a lad or as a man Jesus climbed to the hilltops above the town a marvellous panorama was laid out before and around him. The history of Israel was spread before him. Below the Tabor lay the plains of Esdraelon where Deborah and Barak had destroyed King Jabin's Canaanite army under Sisera with his chariots; there too Gideon had won many of his victories and further west was Megiddo where King Josiah had fallen in disastrous defeat trying to halt an Egyptian invasion. In the valley too was Naboth's vineyard, the place where Jezebel met her death and the home village of Elishah. As eyes lifted higher there was Mount Moriah where Abraham offered up Isaac and over to the west Mount Carmel where Elijah had overthrown the prophets of Baal.

But not only was his and his prophets' history laid out before him the world too unfolded itself before a hilltop in Nazareth. Three great roads skirted it. The great 'way of the sea' which led from Egypt to Damascus with laden caravans moving along it. Then there was the road to the East with its Arabian caravans and

Roman troops marching to the Empire's Eastern frontiers. Finally, there was the hill road south to Jerusalem with the pilgrims on their way to the great festivals. Jesus' home was no backwater. History and the modern world were all around it and its people- the Galileans were a fiercely independent and innovative people delighting in sedition and ever ready to follow any leader who would bring an insurrection. – Not my description but that of a the Roman-Jewish historian Josephus.

At the start of his ministry Jesus was welcomed among his own people and hence he was asked to speak in the Synagogue. And here it began to go wrong Jesus read the Messianic passage from Isaiah pronounced its fulfilment in himself. But where he quoted the Universal love of God shown by Elisha to the Sodomite widow of Zareptah and by Elishah to the Syrian general Naaman, the synagogue Jews were enraged and threw him out. The Kingdom belonged to them as the chosen people whilst the Gentiles were created by God to be the fuel for the fires of hell.

In their reactions we find the most dangerous extreme of the Christian Church, Extreme Protestant Calvinism like the Fundamentalist Sects held this faith of the chosen few – all others are damned- this is echoed in orthodox Judaism in today's Israel and in modern Fundamentalist Islam. This certainty of alone being God's chosen lacks totally the love, the compassion and forgiveness of Christ. It finds no room for, no acceptance of and no desire to welcome back the sinner.

Yet here was Jesus – one of their own – proclaiming the Gospel – the Good News of the Kingdom wherein all who turned to God would find a home and new life, and his own could not accept it.

Mark followed by Matthew places this event later in Jesus ministry when his preaching and healing power were already well known in the region from his work in Capernaum. Equally acceptably they put his rejection at Nazareth down to his being so well known as just a craftsman and they could not accept him as anything more. In such an atmosphere he could not exercise his power to stir men's hearts or heal men's bodies.

Is there not a lesson here for us?

Our churches might be very different places if congregations would only realise or remember that THEY are more than half their sermons.

In an atmosphere of attention and expectancy the poorest effort may light a fire in the listener.

In an atmosphere of critical coldness or bland indifference the most spirit-packed utterance can bounce off deaf ears and fall lifeless to the ground.

Such is the burden of the Nazareth debacle as Mark and Matthew record it and it can be damming enough for many congregations in the church today.

But worse still is the picture raised up by St Luke of a congregation which despises and rejects the outsider whoever he may be – the coloured stranger, the working-class man, the awkward youth, the unmarried mother, the gay or lesbian individual, the physically and mentally handicapped.

We are agents of the Kingdom and have great responsibility in forwarding the work of Christ- of bringing home the lost, the lonely, the awkward, the unloved: In opening the door wide to them we open it to him – in closing it to them we slam it in his face. The Kingdom doors, our door, must be open and welcoming to all.

## 13. Pentecost.

From this dramatic moment at Pentecost with our forty references in the next ten chapters of Acts Luke makes it clear that the early Church is a spirit filled Church and precisely therein lies its power, as the Spirit is shown as the source of guidance to people's actions and decisions: as a  power at work in all the leaders of the Church: as the source of day to day courage: and finally a Spirit the measure of which in a man is conditional by the kind of man he is, the Spirit which God gives to those who obey him.

What exactly happened on the day of Pentecost we really do not know. Luke was not an eyewitness of this decisive moment when the disciples had an experience of the power of the Spirit flooding into their lives such as they never had before.

He describes the disciples speaking in other tongues as the Spirit gave them utterance as speaking in foreign languages. This was totally unnecessary as the audience of Jews and Proselytes gathered for the great feast of Pentecost from all around the Mediterranean world would all speak the Koine, the Greek language which was the lingua franca of their world.

Equally it makes no sense that if all present were hearing the Gospel in their own language there would have been no reason for Peter to start his speech with the words, 'These men are not drunk as you suppose seeing as it is only 9am.'

Quite clearly Luke is describing a phenomenon in the early Church which has never completely passed away. In fact there are present day Congregations who see the gift of speaking in tongues as a necessary proof of Christians being converted and filled with the Holy Spirit. What happened is that people, in a state of ecstasy, began to pour out a flood of unintelligible sounds in no kind of language at all. I have heard it and it certainly is unintelligible. This was/is supposed to be directly inspired by the Spirit of God. Strange as it may sound it was and still is for some Christians a greatly coveted gift. Paul speaks about it in 1 Corinthians 14 and although possessing the gift himself does not approve of it very much except perhaps in private. For the Gospel must be preached in language which the listener can understand and any stranger coming in to meet it in public worship might well think he had arrived in a congregation of madmen or drunkards as the audience thought on the day of Pentecost.

But now we face for ourselves the question should the gift of the Spirit be some dramatic event or experience? Confirmation, Ordination: were these occasions of a dramatic experience of a sudden falling with Divine power? I think not. In my introduction I listed the experience of the early Church of the Holy Spirit at work within individuals, and it is the last which is the key I believe to our experience of the Holy Spirit in our own lives: The measure of the Spirit which a man can possess is conditioned by the kind of man he is for the gift of the Spirit is given by God to those who obey Him.

In Jesus' own words the Spirit whom the Father will send will lead the disciple into all truth and will come as the Comforter, or in more meaningful words the strengthener. When Paul speaks of the gifts of the Spirit he talks of the gifts given to individuals for their own particular form of service be it wisdom, knowledge, healing, preaching, or the gift of discernment. It is one and the same Spirit which gives a different gift to each person; shown in the service for the good of all. He also speaks of the fruits of the Spirit in love, joy, peace, patience, kindness, goodness, faithfulness, humility, and self-control.

All these are given to those who live close to God, striving to walk and live after the pattern of Christ himself. So for you and for me as we seek to follow Christ in our living, to stay close to God in prayer and worship and seek in all things to love our neighbour God will give us his Spirit, not usually in anything dramatic but in enabling us in his service and bringing us evermore closer to himself.

So as we rejoice in the living presence of God's spirit within us let us pray that we may so walk with God that more and more of his Spirit may inform and shape us ever more closely in the pattern and image of our Saviour Jesus Christ.

Amen.

## 14. Go Do Thou Likewise.

During the next few months all our Gospel readings will come from the Gospel of Luke who performs one special service for all of us to ponder and accept, he reminds us of the truth which we all need to learn.

When Jesus wanted to show how the Gospel was to be lived, he picked not God-fearing Jews, but to their indignation those whom they regarded as unclean or outwith the Covenant of God.

The first people – sent by the angels – to visit and worship the unborn Christ were humble shepherds regarded by the Jews as unclean and irreligious.

Then when he answered a plea for help from a Roman centurion- to the Jews the perfect example of the hated oppressive occupying power – who believed that there was no need for Jesus to enter the house when his servant lay sick, just a word would do, Jesus said to those who stood by, 'I have never found such faith, not even in Israel.'

Then he held up an example of great love and penitence the woman of ill repute who anointed his feet and washed them with her tears. To her much was forgiven for she loved much and had performed a service which his host had not had the manners to perform.

Then there came the Samaritan- every bit as hated as the Romans- and rejected as heretical who was yet the one leprosy sufferer who returned to give thanks for his healing.

Finally, there was the better known good Samaritan who gave succour to the bandit-wounded traveller upon whom the priest and the Levite turned their backs in disgust and fear of being made ritually unclean by touching what might be a dead body.

In all these cases Jesus took the sinner, the outcast, the heathen and even the hated enemy as examples of the real love, faith and generosity which was supposed to be the monopoly of the chosen people.

In all these cases Jesus was driving home the truth that we cannot limit the actions of God's spirit to any chosen people and so reject it in others be they Catholics, Muslims, atheists, or society's outcasts.

Wherever and in whomsoever there is charity and love there is God, there the spirit of God is at work. And so, we must confess with shame and humility that all too often we have to be shown the ways of Christ by those who are outside our church.

More important still we need to recognise and affirm the Spirit of God working in others who are not of our faith, race, nationality or social standing and work with them in their furtherance of all that is good.

For Christ's words to the lawyer must always ring in our ears, 'Go and do thou likewise.'

## 15. Friendship.

I have never forgotten an occasion on TV about twenty years ago when on a Sunday evening programme, a Presbyterian minister was asked by his interviewer 'what he valued most in life?' To my surprise he did not answer 'the Church, my faith, the love of God' but quite simply 'friendship'.

Well today we are celebrating the feast of St Barnabas whom I regard as the Patron Saint of friendship. Hence the two passages of scripture which Dulcie read to us and which say a lot about the meaning of friendship and may therefore have something to say to all of us today. Anyway, they are the basis of the thoughts which I want to share with you this morning. I am sure that you are all familiar with the love of David and Jonathan, especially the stories of Jonathan risking his own life in the arrow firing episode to save David from Saul and of David's great lament for Saul and Jonathan after their death in the battle on Mt Gilboa – but this morning's passage I suspect is not so familiar to you.

Yet it gives us certain basic truths about the necessary foundation upon which friendship can be built. Please notice that word built for like that different kind of friendship which we call marriage, all relationships must be worked at if they are to deepen and grow. No relationship can ever stand still, at least not if it is to stand the test of time.

Jonathan gave David two gifts. First, he took off his robe and gave it to David. Then he took off his armour, sword and bow and gave them to David. The Prince took off his royal robes and made himself equal with the shepherd. The warrior divested himself of his arms and made himself vulnerable. I can think of no better symbolism than this to describe the basis of real friendship.

In all friendship there must be equality. Difference of wealth or status or intellect or physical prowess must be laid aside, for genuine friendship can only start when people meet each other quite simply as themselves, without pretence, without any desire for domination, without any need to impress and with no desire to use another.

So much then for the royal clothing! But Jonathan gave away his armour and weapons too. He made himself vulnerable and in this act we see an affirmation of trust. As we all know trust is a risk. It can be abused; confidences can be betrayed; special knowledge can be used against the person who exercises such trust in another. Yet it is only in such a relationship of trust that we can voice some of our deeper hopes, fears, worries and inadequacies which are hidden from all others and perhaps find or give that help and acceptance which can build us up. Equally, only when there is such trust does it become possible to speak hard truths to another which may perhaps be accepted from the lips of one who speaks out of caring but will never be accepted from anyone else on whose lips such truths will only be heard as malice or condemnation.

Jonathan took off his royal robes. Jonathan took off arms and armour and he gave them to David. The root of friendship and of any deep relationship lies in the ability to give of ourselves to another. In friendships that fail, if you look closely, you will find that on one side or the other or both giving has ceased. And it is all summed up in the statement that Jonathan loved David as he loved himself.

Barnabas takes us another stage on our exploration of friendship. He had become a very close friend of Paul in the first days of Paul's ministry but the Apostles did not want to know Paul when he went to Jerusalem. No way would they accept into their fellowship that ex-persecutor of the Church. They did not believe that the leopard could change his spots. So Barnabas put his own head on the block and brought Paul in to them and openly expressed his trust in Paul, his guarantee of Paul's new and marvellous work for God, at the risk of being rejected himself. But for Barnabas one wonders how different might have been the story of the greatest missionary of the early Church.

But Barnabas was to face a worse test yet. The very young Mark who accompanied Paul and Barnabas on their first missionary journey dropped out halfway through because it was too much for him and he was neither old nor strong enough to cope. Three years later he asked to join them on a second missionary journey and Paul turned him down flat. Once a coward and deserter always a coward and deserter. This time it was the youngster who needed Barnabas' support. When he stood up for Mark Paul told him that if that was how he felt he could jolly well go with Mark and he, Paul, would do very well without either of them. So, Barnabas sadly left his oldest friend and went with the younger one who needed him and according to tradition after working with Barnabas in Cyprus went on to found the North African Church.

I wonder how many ex-prisoners or young offenders' lives might be very different if there were more St Barnabas' around today?

We come now to today's Gospel. Christ said, 'Greater love hath no man than this- that a man lay down his life for his friends.' He said it and then he did it. Here is the ultimate giving. He then went on to say to his disciples, 'I do not call you servants but I call you friends because you know what I am doing. And you are my friends if you do what I command you and share in my work of loving'. Here we see friendship not as an end in itself but as a creative activity, bearing fruit- fruit that will last.

Yes, we all know a real friendship grows and works inwards for personal security, sense of value and happiness but it must also grow outwards.

Inwardly a deep friendship enriches the life of both individuals as selfishness succumbs to selflessness; as mutual self-knowledge and acceptance grow; as loneliness develops into close companionship and as problems are shared and faced and often overcome or more patiently borne than would have been possible on our own. Outwardly too real friendship can and must change us.

Building on the relationship we have with our closest friend or friends we are enabled to create new relationships with a wider circle of people.

For just as we must share our experience of the love and strength we find in our relationship with God: So too we must take the gifts of acceptance and being valued as we are (rather than for who or what we are) of trust and loyalty of support and caring in good times and in bad and offer them to others. There may be no response or even rejection but we will be enriched and grow ourselves in the process.

Let me end with the words from the poem Footprints in the Sand by an unknown writer.

The Lord answered, 'My precious child, I love you and I would never leave you. During your times of trial, when you see only one set of footprints, that's when I am carrying you.'

If you change the word Lord to friend do you not then have a perfect description of true friendship, of that deep companionship and sharing on the path of life in which now and again the one will have to carry the other?

So, let us thank God today for the treasure of friendships, of varying depth, which are ours, let us pray that they may become more selfless and rich in joy and sharing and pray too that we may learn to stretch out our hands in friendship to more of those around us and especially to those whose need is greatest.

Amen.

# 16. Transfiguration.

Three times Peter, James and John were alone with Jesus at a tremendous moment: The first had been when he raised Jairus' daughter from the dead: The third would be his agony in the garden of Gethsemane: His second was the scene of his Transfiguration high up on Mount Hermon in the north of Galilee. Only six days before had come Peter's confession, 'Thou art the Christ', at Caesarea Philippi and Jesus' first clear statement that he must face death in Jerusalem.

Here on the cloud-shrouded heights of the Mount Hermon comes a moment of the vision of Christ in glory and the decisive moment as Christ makes his irrevocable decision to set off south for Jerusalem and the Cross.

The passage is so full of symbolism for those who are steeped in the Old Testament that I can only take some aspects today.

The faithful there were granted the momentary glimpse of Christ in his glory. On his right and left stood Moses and Elijah, to the Jews the two greatest figures in Jewish history.

On one side Moses who led the Jews out of their living death of slavery in Egypt in the Exodus on their way to the promised land which he was to see from the hills of Moab to the east of Jordan but was not himself to enter. Moses who had given his people God's laws in the ten commandments and hence a standard of morality far in advance of that of any other in the ancient world.

On the other side stood Elijah, held to be the greatest of the prophets through whom the voice of God spoke to men with unique directness. Behind Elijah stood, unseen, those other prophets who had made special revelations of the nature of God: Amos - God's passionate concern for justice. Hosea- God's capacity for forgiveness. Isaiah – A God who suffers on his people's behalf. Jeremiah – the law of God which should be written in people's hearts rather than on tables of stone. Ezekiel – who had a vision of God's capacity to raise the dead. All these deepened the vision of the nature of God, yet to the Jews Elijah stood on the summit of prophecy.

Moses and Elijah stood there talking to Jesus of his exodus. In the Gospel the words have been paraphrased beyond recognition: AV: of his decease which he should accomplish at Jerusalem, but the Greek word had but one connotation: the departure of Israel from Egypt into the unknown way of the desert which was to lead them to the promised land, a journey which had to be made in utter trust of God. So Moses and Elijah were speaking to Jesus of this exodus in faith, leading God's people from a greater bondage than that of

Egypt through his death and resurrection to the Kingdom of Heaven.

Then a cloud covered the three figures and there was the voice 'This is my son whom I have chosen, listen to him.' A.V's more telling 'Hear ye Him.' When the cloud lifted the Jesus they knew stood alone. The two pillars of the Old Testament were gone.

'Hear ye Him.' The old Mosaic law was gone as Christ brought the new commandment 'that ye love one another as I have loved you.' The old law as Paul wrote, so truly, could only convict man of sin, the new law could lead to LIFE. The old prophecy could only give man a glimpse of God, Jesus himself was the image of God, 'he who hath seen me hath seen the Father...I am come not to destroy but to fulfil the Law and the Prophets.' The days of the Law and the Prophets, of Moses and Elijah were over for now God had spoken through his Son.

The chosen three were granted a vision of Christ in glory which they could only understand and speak about after the Resurrection, yet which must surely in the days to come have been an inspiration to them, a confirmation of the glory of God and the power of God and indeed the reality of God to shine in their hearts and minds in times of doubt and danger.

So _finally,_ for us there is the same truth which meant that Peter could not build three tabernacles and stay there. Back down the mountain they must go together to face the crowds, the epileptic boy whom the other disciples had been unable to cure and the journey to Jerusalem, to Gethsemane, to Golgotha and to the empty tomb and beyond.

So it is and must be for us. At odd moments in all our lives we have/we are granted a glimpse or glimpses of the glory of God when we know that our faith is true; when we are certain of the love of God, when we feel very close to Heaven. Yet we cannot stay in those moments for ever. We are given them to be a light, to be an assurance, to which we must hold firm in an everyday world, an everyday life which so often can make peace and joy - yes even faith to flee from us. So as we give thanks for this wonderful Feast of the Transfiguration vouchsafed just to the eyes of Peter, James, and John: Let us pray that we may know our own lesser moments of vision to be the truth and that they may sustain _us_ in _our_ daily living.

Amen.

## 17. Servant.

Jesus had a great capacity for immensely hard and infuriating ways of attacking and shaming the self-righteous and oppressive scribes, Pharisees, and teachers of the law. In chapter 23 of Matthew's Gospel, 'woe to you teachers of the law and Pharisees. How do you expect to escape from being condemned to Hell?' This was plain speaking with a vengeance.

But also, he shamed the powerful and self-righteous Jewish leaders in other words and actions:

'The parable of the good Samaritan – an outcast in Jewish eyes showed up the callousness of priest and Levite who passed by on the other side to avoid becoming ritually unclean – and showed that it was the outcast who by showing mercy did the will of God.

Turning to the Jews after the healing of the Centurion's servant he told them straight 'I have not found so great faith, no not in Israel.'

Coming thirsty to the well at Sychar he asked the Samaritan woman to give him a drink.

Along with his habit of eating and drinking with sinners he proclaimed again and again by word and deed that the so-called outcasts were closer to the Kingdom of Heaven than the self-important and upright Jews.

James emphasises this in today's epistle which I won't repeat since I am sure you heard and took his words to heart – especially that judgement 'If you treat people according to their outward appearance you are guilty of sin.'

But in the Gospel, we find Jesus speaking ever more forcefully- not this time to the Jews but to his own disciples. The occasion was caused by the wife of Zebedee's request that her sons should have the places of honour in Jesus' Kingdom. Despite Jesus' negative answer the other ten disciples were furious...so Jesus called them all together and uttered those familiar words: 'You know that the rulers of the heathen have a power over them and the leaders have complete authority'.... think of modern tyrannical dictators, millionaire banking chiefs, top business tycoons, our council bosses, and any other important overbearing people you know.

Jesus words now strike home 'This however is not the way it shall be among you. IF one of you wants to be great he must be the servant of the rest - and if one of you wants to be first he must be your slave like the Son of Man who did not come to be served, but to serve and give his life to redeem many people.

To drive home his message Jesus took contemporary examples and so before I conclude I would like to do the same.

Round about 7am a slightly overweight yellow jacketed figure sets off from the north car park with brushes, spade, and barrow to clear the kerbs and pavements of Dunkeld and through Birnam. The man of course is the street sweeper and his name is Steve. Most people, like I suspect the Priest and Levite, give him a fairly wide berth and forget him.

A year or two back during our Meeting Place get together in the Duchess Anne and - perhaps the snow was making him run late - he came trudging down the cross past the bank and I went out and invited him in for a coffee. His reply 'I can't do that, if the Gaffer sees me knock off he'll give me hell.'

It took at least a month before he gave in. He parks his bin in one of the northside archways- it is now 8.00am- I make him a coffee and we sit down and talk. I hear about his ailments, his painful right hand the wasps in the local bins and how cold he is and how good are his short breaks with his family. As I boil the kettle he is, without being asked, already humping tables and chairs ready for the social meeting.

In the summer months he reaches St Mary's some time after 11.00am and after more persuasion he comes in and sits down leaving in all humility at least one chair's space with the nearest person.

So, day by day feeling well or not so well be there snow, rain, leaves, detritus of our leaving the servant of our community goes on unnoticed, un-thanked and little rewarded.

To the Gaffer, to the community he is just the 'street sweeper' but as servant to us all highly to be rewarded by God.

I don't know how proud, how influential, how rich, how powerful, how important any of us, any Christian may feel – until we become servants to others and to those in need, we are a long way from the Kingdom of God.

How good is it to know that our sovereign at her Coronation as head of Church and State and Commonwealth promises 'I will serve my people all my life.'

The head of the Catholic Church, the Pope, his proudest title is to be 'Servus Servorum Dei' - servant of the servants of God. Jesus the Son of God our Lord and Saviour promises as St Luke records his words:

'I am among you as one who serves hence the washing of the disciples' feet. I am among you as one who serves. Go do thou likewise.'

Amen.


## 18. Jeremiah

For months now our O.T. readings have been from Jeremiah who to my mind was the greatest of the Jewish prophets for his compassionate love for his own people – his unflinching stand against evil living and idolatrous worship – his sufferings for that stand and his clear political vision and his understanding of a true relationship with God, and how suffering could purge the nation's sins for God would never desert his people. He lived in troubled times.

Assyria had destroyed the Northern kingdom of Samaria and now Judah was next in the mighty jaws of Assyria soon to be defeated and destroyed by Babylon to the north and King Neco's Egypt in the South. Judah had to be subservient to one or the other or be crushed utterly.

Jermiah owed much to his northern predecessors: Amos with his unyielding passion for justice: Hosea with his unfailing belief in God's love for his backsliding people and as a young man he would have experienced the religious revival under King Josiah who brought in the reforms of the Book of Deutoronomy/ Deutoros nomos:the second law – and one of the very few kings who is recorded in II Kings and II Chronicles as 'doing that which was right in the eyes of the Lord.'

Jeremiah's call came in the 13<sup>th</sup> year of Josiah's 31 year reign and like so many other prophets before him who saw the probable painful and harsh realities of such a call, he was loath to accept it: 'Sovereign Lord I am too young, I don't know how to speak.' 'But the Lord said – do not say you are too young – go to the people I send you to and tell them everything I tell you to say. Do not be afraid of them: I will be with you to protect you. I the Lord have spoken. Listen Jeremiah! Everyone in this land will be against you: The Kings, the officials, the Priests and the people: But I will give you the strength to resist them.'

For 18 years all was well but in 609BC King Neco of Egypt marched through the land to aid ailing Assyria against rising power of Babylon and Josiah tried to stop him at Megiddo but was defeated and killed. King Nebuchadnezzar crushed the Egyptians at Carchemish 4 years later, became master of the Mediterranean world and everything changed. Under Jehoiakim and Zedekiah who tried to play Egypt (their closest neighbours) off against Babylon with disastrous results Judah went back to the old ways of injustice, exploitation of the poor and false pagan religion of Baal worship – and now Jeremiah's travails began.

Jeremiah now preached against evil doing against ever increasing opposition – facing death threats in his home town of Anathoth and in Jerusalem and above all rejection of his cry that Judah must be subservient to Babylon or face destruction. The personal pain was colossal 'The pain! I cannot bear the pain! My heart is beating wildly, one disaster follows another, the whole country is left in ruins. My sorrow cannot be healed. I am sick at heart, listen! Throughout the land I hear my people crying out. I wish my head were a well of water and my eyes a fountain of tears so that I could cry day and night for my people who have been killed.'

Yet he still spoke out his twofold message of turning back to God and subservience to Babylon or face destruction. For this he was beaten and put in chains but released, in 592 Jerusalem was taken and many leading people deported including King Jehoiakim. Now Zedekiah was king but nothing changed and Jeremiah was temporarily imprisoned again. In prison he got his scribe to write a scroll which proclaimed disaster unless the people turned back to God. He was to read it to the temple from which Jeremiah was forever banned. The temple officials took it to King Zedekiah who cut it to pieces and burnt it.

Once again Nebuchadnezzar laid siege to Jerusalem. Jeremiah refused to change his message in a personal interview with the king and was locked up and fed bread until supplies ran out. Then the officials demanded

Jeremiah's death for wrecking the soldiers morale and he was flung into a dry well to sink the mud and the dirt. But Zedekiah had him rescued because part of his mind knew Jeremiah was right yet he dared not act. In 589BC the city fell Zedekiah witnessed the execution of his sons, was himself blinded and along with all except the poorest in the land taken in exile in Babylon. Jeremiah who had bought a parcel of land to proclaim his faith that God would in due time restore his broken people, refused to leave and stayed under the protection of Governor Gedaliah at Mizpah. When Gedaliah was murdered, fearful of reprisals, the local Jews fled to Egypt taking an unwilling Jeremiah with them never to return. But as he had promised 50 years later when the Persian King Cyrus defeated Babylon the exiled Jews were sent home to rebuild their temple and their homes.

Great was his heart of compassion and love for his people sinful though they were. Great was his courage in continuing to preach the truth as he saw it. Great was his unwavering faith that however God allowed the chosen people to suffer for their sins yet he would never desert them. And finally great was his insight into religion which I have not mentioned until now. In chapter 31 he wrote of the New Covenant which God would make with his people. It would be a Covenant not written on stone or tablets to be obeyed to avoid God's wrath but written in men's hearts as a loving response to God's love.

This surely is the prefiguring of the Gospel as we know it. The Christian life is not primarily the keeping of an external law in fear. It is the weak, often sinful man's attempt to love God and others as God loves us. Jeremiah's people could not see or accept this, pray God you and I can!

## 19. The Shema

'What commandment in the law is the greatest?' So Jesus is asked in today's Gospel. In Matthew as read today it sounds as though the Pharisees are once again hoping to attack Jesus. In Mark however it is asked by a Scribe out of gratitude that Jesus had confronted the Pharisees and Herodians as we heard last week. Then in Luke it is Jesus' response to a Scribe who earnestly sought the truth and led to the parable of the Good Samaritan in response to 'But who is my neighbour?'

We start every service with a quote from the Shema the sentence with which every synagogue service also always begins. It is so called for Shema is the imperative of the Hebrew verb to hear...Hear O Israel the Lord thy God is the only God and thou shalt love the Lord God with your whole heart, mind, soul, and strength. Here was and is the foundation stone of Jewish and our monotheistic faith. For the Jew this demand from Deuteronomy 6, is contained in the phylacteries which were little leather boxes worn on wrists and forehead when the Jews were at prayer. It was also contained in a little cylindrical box called the Mezuzah which was and still is fixed to the door of every Jewish home and also every room within it to remind the Jew of his/her commitment to God in every coming out and going in. But to this Jesus added the command 'Thou shalt love thy neighbour as thyself.'

And so our service starts each Sunday with this double reminder of our whole obligation and duty as Christians. Jesus put these two together in asserting that the only way anyone can prove that they love God is by showing their love for mankind through loving their neighbour.

It is important, indeed vital, that we note in which order the commandments come. Love of God first, love of man second. And this so because the second is not in our nature but springs from the first: the love of God, the command of God – if you love me you will keep my commandments. You must love one another as I have loved you.

This love springs from love of God, obedience to his word and through the power and grace of the spirit of God in us.

I have just been re-reading the books of anthropologist Robert Ardrey as he debunks the humanist's fallacy of man's innate goodness and Freud's theory that all man's behaviour has a sexual basis. He traces our slow million-year advance from our primate ancestors bringing with us those instincts and learning which alone enabled homo sapiens to survive in a hostile environment.

These basic instincts include the following:

Hostility in defence of our family, group, nation, and territory against our neighbours.

The drive for dominance within our family or society.

The use of weapons in a predatory carnivore's way of life.

The driving out of the young upstart or rebel within our society to fight their own way out with the family or society.

You only have to look honestly at yourself. At our national histories, our class warfare, our criminal gangs, our capacity for murder and mayhem to know that this is the truth about who and what we are.

We all carry the legacy of our evolutionary past ingrained in our innermost being. 'Made in the image of God' is a statement of possibility, a promise of potential if we were redeemed.

This the source – the reality behind the Pauline contrast of the flesh – meaning natural man and the Spirit meaning man touched and redeemed by the Grace of God.

It is only when we give ourselves totally to God that we may find the grace and the power to love and serve our neighbours be he an enemy, a criminal, a totally different coloured national, be he seemingly unteachable, unreformable, totally alien in his thoughts and behaviour.... I needn't go on with this list need I. We all know of the deep down resentments, anger, even hatred latent within ourselves.

It is only when we give ourselves wholly to God and seek and receive of his Holy Spirit that we may approach in and with Jesus and the Saints the capacity to love our neighbours and so to change our families, our societies, our world.

Amen.

## 20. Remembrance Sunday.

I was only six years old when my father who was a barrister disappeared into the army in 1939 and spent the whole of the second world war in India. He returned home all too briefly and then disappeared again for another year as an army lawyer for the war crimes trials in Germany from which he returned with grey hair at the age of forty and would never say a word about the horrors which had been revealed in the trials of Nazi war criminals.

His silence was enough to bring home to me the horrors of war and the reason relations and friends of the family had died to fight an evil which had to be stopped. It was a terrible war but the first world war was infinitely worse. With 10 million killed and 21 million wounded (five times that of the second world war casualties) it was a scale that defies one's comprehension. There was hardly a family in the land that did not lose a loved one and nowhere is that truer than here in Scotland. When I stood on Thursday at the war memorial in Birnam – there was a roll of 75 dead from a community of perhaps 500 people. Sacrifice and loss on such a scale cannot be forgotten.

Those of you born since those two wars live in a world where television now brings home to you the terrible evils of today's wars. Live pictures come to you of Northern Ireland,

Ethiopia, the Sudan and Bosnia and maybe you ask, 'Why O why cannot someone put a stop to such things?'

You can understand why it should be felt that such forces of evil must be opposed by force and at almost any cost. Every Remembrance Sunday the nation remembers the terrible cost that was paid in the two World Wars and other recent conflicts like the Falklands to preserve human freedom.

The poppies which you wear are a symbol of remembrance taken from the poppies which had filled the fields of Flanders before the terrible trench warfare and the years of attrition in World War 1 turned the countryside into a muddy wasteland of death.

After the war, a grateful nation rewarded its top generals with important positions, with one exception. That exception was Field Marshal Sir Douglas Haig, a Scotsman, and the nation could not forgive him as supreme British commander in Flanders throughout those terrible battles. In his simple Calvinistic faith he had been sure that God was with him and would grant us victory- whatever the cost. So he retired with his Earldom to Bemersyde. Yet he was the one who acted after the war on behalf of all the crippled and injured. He initiated the sale of red poppies to raise money for those who lived but had paid a terrible price physically or mentally for their service. Still today it is the Earl Haig Poppy fund which receives your money for servicemen and their families in need from the world wars and more recent conflicts. So your poppies are symbols of Remembrance and they are also symbols of grateful compassion. A compassion which is also so finely shown in the work of the British Legion.

*Remembrance and Compassion.*

I would like to think though that you will regard your poppies as symbols of something else too, symbols of your commitment to work for peace and reconciliation.

The roots of war do not in the end lie in past history or national and tribal leaders' decisions. They lie in the hearts and minds of individuals who are ruled by hatred or envy or greed or desire for revenge for past wrongs- real or imagined. Given enough such individuals – then and only then can politicians or leaders start the assault on others which leads to war.

If this is true of war, it is also true of peace. Peace too starts with the individual. In our first reading you heard the dream of the peace-loving Micah at a time when Assyrian armies threatened to attack and overwhelm his country. It was a lovely dream of the weapons of war being transformed into agricultural implements so that his people could live and work their fields in peace and without fear.

But it was not enough to dream and be a peace-lover. Christ said that the blessed ones were not peace-lovers but rather peacemakers. Since peace making starts with the individual – as did the Gospel of love and forgiveness, with Christ who laid down his life for our own peace – it starts with each of us.

It starts as we purge our minds and lives of the anger and violence, the vengefulness and ill-will which dwells in each and every one of us. As we learn to care and to forgive, to be reconciled with and to understand our neighbour, we become instruments of God's peace. The dream, our dream may become a reality in our world as like Christ we give of ourselves to and for others.

So when you go home put your poppies somewhere where you can see them every day so that as today, they remind us of those who gave their lives for our freedom and remind us too of our duty to care with compassion and generosity for those who have given their health for our freedom:

So also day by day we may be reminded that in our daily living we are to be peace makers in our own communities and in that living may in some small measure share in the sacrifice made measurable in the words-

'When you go home tell them and say for your tomorrow, we gave our today.'

Amen.

*Act of Penitence.*

Oh Lord you created mankind to live in harmony with your creation and in love for one another. For our sin which has defaced your world and brought untold sufferings upon your people through carnage and devastation of war, forgive us O Lord.

For human and national greed, rivalry and dreams of conquest, forgive us O Lord.

For racial intolerance which has led us to the evils of the holocaust, ethnic cleansing and terrorism, forgive us O Lord.

For blasphemous bigotry which has led us to seek to vindicate a religious creed by use of the sword, forgive us O Lord.

For the misuse of our creative powers which has led us to inflict the modern horrors of nuclear weapons, napalm, the gas chambers and chemical warfare upon countless innocent men, women and children, forgive us O Lord.

For the evil within each of us as we give way to anger, malice, revenge and hatred, forgive us O Lord.

O heavenly father whose son died for our sins praying 'father forgive them, they know not what they do'.

Bring all people and nations to a full knowledge and abhorrence of the evil of war, - bring us to repent of our strife and violence – Forgive us the evil we do and have done and make us instruments of your peace.

We ask this through the same your son, Jesus Christ our Lord.

Amen.

### Intercession.

O Lord our God we give you thanks this day for the remembrance of those who served their country and laid down their lives for our sakes. We pray that their sacrifice may not be in vain and that they may rest in peace. Lord in your mercy.

(Response)

We pray for all those living who still bear in their minds and bodies the injuries and scars of their service. Lord in your mercy.

(Response)

We pray for all those who live with the pain and loneliness of bereavement of loved ones taken from them in war. Lord in your mercy.

(Response)

We pray for those who as a result of war live in destitution, bereft of homes and the bare necessities of life and helpless before the ever-present fear of debt through disease and starvation. Lord in your mercy.

*(Response)*

We pray for the armed forces of our country in their role as peacekeepers in Northern Ireland and many other corners of the world. Lord in your mercy

*(Response)*

We pray for ourselves that you will enlarge our compassion for all who suffer; strengthen our resolve to live and work for peace; and help us to obey your command to love our neighbours as ourselves. Lord in your mercy.

*(Response)*

And let us sum up then our prayer in the words which Christ himself has taught us saying: Our Father.......

# 21. Pain as Prayer.

We're into November, green plants are blackened in the frosts, the leaves fall everywhere and damp gets into our very bones. It is a time of increasing aches and pains.

As I look around this congregation I think of Barbara with her neck and back very painful after a fall on the ice, I think of John whose arm was broken by a careless driver and has just had to be set a second time and I think of Bob who has had to go through a double operation and been hit by flu at the same time. Their pain and discomfort are all too obvious.

But they are not alone are they? We are all growing older and nearly all of us in this congregation are living with permanent or recurring ailments and are no stranger to physical pain or disability.

I suppose our first reaction, with Job, is to ask why? What have I done to deserve this? Surely it is not a punishment for sin!

There were no answers to his questions, he was a good man, and in the story all was well in the end. But it is not like that in real life and we know that the question 'why me?' has no answer.

I suppose one second reaction is one of anger, we curse God or providence for our suffering and often take it out on those around us. But we know such rage is futile: it is wrong and it is harmful.

Our third reaction is perhaps one of resignation, of opting out of all we can on the grounds of incapacity and in search of sympathy, or even wallow in self-pity. But this too we find to be a profitless and soul-destroying experience.

Perhaps mostly we turn to the old stoic ethic. We must just bear our suffering with all the patience and dignity that we can. We will hide our pain from others and we will not allow it to control our lives or burden theirs if we can help it. There is a courage and almost a nobility in this ethic, yet in the end it is sterile, although at our level this is how we should treat it.

But can there be nothing more than hiding the pain with the smile, the courage, the lack of complaint and lack of self-pity such action requires? As Christians we have to say yes, o yes there is.

First let me tell you of Elisabeth, I cannot remember her surname but she lived a few doors up from my digs in my first curacy in Welling. I used to take her communion. She had been in bed ever since a German bomb had blown up her home and husband and damaged her back that she could only move her head and her arms. Her working daughter looked after her and the front door was always open so that visitors could enter during the daytime.

I never heard Elisabeth complain although there were certainly bad days when she was very tired and obviously in great discomfort. The strange thing was that she never talked about herself but instead got me talking about my frustrations and problems and then sent me away feeling all the better for meeting her. After all my troubles were so insignificant compared to hers. In due course I found that she had many other parishioners who came to visit her, found themselves airing their troubles and left feeling better and more able to cope.

I very soon realised that in her acceptance of her own disability she had found a wealth of compassion and understanding for others and been enabled to give them something of her strength. Yet there had to be more to it than that and it was only after three years that I plucked up the courage to ask her about this.

It was then that she preached to me the last part of this sermon which I am now preaching to you.

She said I think that any power I have comes because 'I make my bad times prayer.'

'I make my bad times prayer.'

Do you remember Isaiah's description of the suffering servant whom the church has always seen as a prefiguring of Christ? 'He was wounded for our transgressions and by his stripes we are healed.'

In the creed we say that 'for us men and for our salvation Christ made man, suffered under Pontius Pilate and was crucified.' Do you recall how often St Paul glories in <u>his</u> sufferings on behalf of his fellow Christians?

There is a special power in suffering which is accepted and offered up for others. When we know and believe this, we can then find a creative purpose and value in our own individual suffering.

It is easy enough Sunday by Sunday to run through some list of sufferers  in the intercessions and the same is true in our private prayer and it costs us nothing even though it is right that we should pray and true that the more earnestly we so pray the more we open up our sensitivity towards others, our power of compassion, and the springs of action to meet the needs of others.

But beyond this lies the possibility of offering up our own pain and suffering as prayer on behalf of others. How God uses such prayer we may never know this side of the grave. The supreme power of self- sacrifice is a mystery like the Cross of Christ but it is a power in which we share when we learn to offer our pain in intercession for others, when as Elisabeth said, 'we make our bad times prayer.'

Because we are human we <u>will</u> always have the moment when we curse our suffering, when we question God's love, when we feel bitter and sorry for ourselves.

Most of the time we will try to bear our pain stoically and by God's grace fight its power to create bitterness and resentment and complaining.

But as Christians we can and must go further. There is so much suffering in the world, close to us and far away, and we feel powerless to change it. Yet if we can offer our suffering to God in union with the suffering of Christ on behalf of others, we are privileged to be offering costly prayer and God will use it, even though we know not how or where.

Sometimes we can offer our suffering for specific people whom we know. Sometimes for those who cry out to us from daily paper or television set. Sometimes for more general needs like world peace or other concerns.

In this way our pain becomes creative instead of destructive. In this way, as we say in the Prayer of Consecration, we offer unto God ourselves: our souls and bodies: to be a living sacrifice and to share in Christs own world redeeming offering of himself.

As I said earlier it is not for us to know just how God will use our offering of ourselves when we make our bad times prayer, but there is also a reward for us. Through the offering God will enable us to grow in our one-ness with his suffering world and he will deepen in us a serenity and the certainty which Paul states in the Epistle to the Romans in the great prayer at the end of chapter 8 which ends, I am convinced that there is nothing in all creation that can separate us from our love of God.

We can all join Christ in Gethsemane and at Golgotha, his body broken for us his blood shed for us, and Elisabeth in her bed is willing in that creative response to suffering which makes us one with Christ and so channels God's healing power.

We too can say 'I will make _my_ bad times prayer.'

Amen

# 22. All Saints.

In sixteen years at Christ's Hospital, I was in our great chapel more times than I can begin to count and, like everyone who has ever entered the building, could never fail to be aware of the sixteen great murals of Brangwyn which ran around the walls above the serried ranks of facing pews.

The murals were huge, raw in execution and powerful. They portrayed an historical series of the Saints and heroes of the Christian Church.

There was Peter preaching at Pentecost, Stephen the first martyr being stoned, Paul's Damascus road conversion, his shipwreck, and his arrival at Rome. Then came the first English martyr St Alban. Next, as was appropriate in a great school with a terrific musical tradition, were the scholar Augustine and Father of Church music Ambrose. These eight, line the Northern wall. Along the Southern wall came the British missionaries Patrick, Columba, Aiden, and Wilfred preaching to the South Saxons of Sussex. Then the years run on to Caxton with his printing press giving bibles for all followed by the missionary bishop John Selwyn and next to him the bishop Elliot presenting bibles to the Mohicans who, I am sure could not read a single word of them. So, before us day by day, as often as we entered our great chapel was this pictorial record of the

Saints and heroes of the Christian Church who by their lives and deaths, by their preaching and scholarship, by their trade and devotion lived and proclaimed the Gospel of God's love.

Now those of you who have been counting will have noticed that I have only mentioned fifteen of the sixteen murals.

The sixteenth is very special. It shows a back street in London, typifying Christ's Hospital's origins under Edward VI as a school for the poor of London, and in that street rather like an original Sankey and Moody scene is an incredible ugly hunch-backed street organist with huge, gnarled fingers playing hymns whilst two tired looking men in surplices and a wicked looking little urchin in similar garb who, I always thought, was about to get a right clip on the ear from the nearer singer. There they are, singing the Lord's praise to an audience who look as ugly and disinterested as it is possible to look. It even appeared that tomato and mud was about to begin!

What on earth, you may well be asking yourselves, is such an unlikely quartet doing on the final picture in Brangwyn's great pageant of Saints and heroes of the Christian Church?

Well today is All Saints and to me that last picture more than all the rest brings home, and always has, the truth of this great festival.

In fact, it carries a double message for me and I hope the memory of it may for you too.

First, where are the Saints of God? The answer in all ages is that they are all around us. The Church has canonised many of the most famous but left unrecognised a countless multitude of ordinary and unknown men, women, and children whose lives have reflected the glory of God's love and whose goodness, devotion, witness, endurance, and sufferings; whose joy and love have reflected that of their saviour Jesus Christ.

Second, who are the Saints of God? The answer as St Paul writes so often to those who he calls the Saints, are those who are called to be Saints meaning all the ministers of the Churches which he founded...and us! You and I are called to be Saints. Each one of us is called so to surrender ourselves to God, to doing his will and to loving his people that our lives may reflect his love and truth and glory in the world today.

All Saints then is a double festival: It is one of rejoicing in that multitude of God's chosen who have come from every walk of society whose achievements and sacrifices and love have been widely or locally known and who have gone before us as lights of the world in their several generations.

We rejoice in the challenge of our own individual calling to be members of that great multitude which no man can number, that multitude who have in the past and who do today praise God in their worship, in the quality of their living and loving and in their acceptance of the love and forgiveness of God and his power which can transform any sinner into one of his Saints.

Brangwyn left the best to the last because the last is so clearly everyman, and everyman is or so clearly could be you and me – God help us.

## 23. The Power of Prayer

This is a difficult time for the disciples halfway between the Resurrection and Ascension. Christ appears to the disciples in the upper room and in Galilee and to others: himself and alive and they are witnesses to his rising from the dead.

So perhaps it is not too surprising that our Gospel takes us back to the morning of the last supper and to Jesus' promise that he will return and prepare a place for them with his Father.

So, Thomas' bafflement and request to show where he was going and Philip's request to show them the Father so that they might believe and understand! Jesus makes it plain that in Him they see the Father for the two are one.

A short while later comes the disciples' bafflement over Christ's statement of a little while of seeing him and not seeing him because he was returning to his Father.

All this was looking to those forty days, in whose midst we are now of the Resurrection appearances until the Ascension and then the first of Pentecost, the coming and empowering of the Holy Spirit.

And so, we come to the final verses of today's Gospel and two tremendous promises.

1: 'Whoever believes in me will do what I do, yes he will do even greater things because I am going to the Father.

Most certainly in the early days the early Church possessed the power of working healing cures, as Paul states in 1 Corinthians, the different gifts of people who had the gift of a power of healing. And then as James urged that when any Christian was sick the elders should pray over him and anoint him with oil bringing healing.

Yet surely this is hardly a doing of even greater things than Jesus did in his healing ministry. Yet as time has gone on man has more and more learned to conquer disease. Today the surgeon and physician with new skills and techniques have powers to which the ancient world would have seemed miraculous and even Godlike.

And while there may be a long way to go yet to storm the citadels of pain and disease the salient fact is that the healing ministry and worldwide mission has always grown and spread through the Christian Church and has reached out into the world of medicine and to the lives of all kinds of men and women, monastic, missionary: International caring people giving their lives to the curing of disease and relief of pain.

Whether they acknowledge it or not Jesus is even now saying to people that their fellows must be helped and healed and it is his spirit which has been behind the conquest of disease. And it is indeed true that man can do things nowadays which in Jesus' time no one could have dreamt of as possible.

2: But when we come to the second promise at the end of today's Gospel: 'I will do whatever you ask in my name so that the Father's glory will be shown through the son. If you ask for anything in my name, I will do it!!'

This promise I for one and perhaps some of you find to be the most difficult passage or promise in all scripture.

So, to my choice of today's Psalm which may cause discomfort that so much of my prayer for those I know and love, for myself, for the suffering sinful world seems to remain unanswered.

And here I do not know what to say to you. I do indeed know of miracles of healing and conversions directly linked with prayer including that of the healing rooms here in St Mary's.

I do believe most firmly that my prayer which reaches out into the wide world brings God's power into the lives and service of those working for health, healing, and peace in regions where I cannot go.

I do believe that God's answer to some of my prayers for others comes back to me from Christ in the challenge, 'You act yourself and become my instrument in answering your prayer.'

I do believe in the Christian's duty to pray widely in love and compassion for the whole world of men, women, and children with all their sufferings, problems, and sin and to try when praying for others to see them with the eyes of Christ and to pray in the name of Jesus in prayer that must always end: Thy will be done.

From there I can take you no further. The promise is there and how God will fulfil that promise I cannot tell but I do know that prayer is the most powerful weapon that you and I have in releasing the power of God in Christ and the Holy Spirit into our lives and those of others whom we may never even see or know.

I want to end this collection of sermons with my personal mantra from the Prophet Micah

*I have showed thee o man what the Lord doth require of thee. To deal justly and to love mercy and to walk humbly with thy God.*

This, I hope, has been the pattern of my life.

Rev. Ian Atkinson

May 2022.

Printed in Great Britain
by Amazon